PRAISE

"For any adviser who is looking to build a true business—as opposed to managing a basic practice—Erin Botsford's book is a must-read. Erin is one of the wealth management industry's best examples of how an adviser with a CEO-state of mind can ignite structured, strategic and sustainable growth. Her latest book should be on the desk of any adviser who is looking for a plan and a process that can propel their firm to the next level."

—**Mark Bruno,** Associate Publisher, *InvestmentNews*

"It's not often that you find a successful person willing to reveal the secret sauce of their success. But that is what Erin Botsford has done her latest book *Seven Figure Firm—How to Build a Financial Services that Grows Itself.* Often financial advisers struggle to transform their successful practice into a self-sustaining business. Ms. Botsford explains how she did it and offers practical guidelines of how to replicate her success, right down to the details of where to seat clients in an initial meeting and why it is important to keep track of their coffee, tea, or coke preference. In an era of robo-advisors, building a brand to differentiate your services is key and establishing systems to provide a consistently superior client experience is the equivalent of building the golden arches of a successful financial services firm."

—**Mary Beth Franklin,** CFP, Contributing Editor, *Investment News*

"Erin Botsford has never accepted the concept of a glass ceiling and as a result, she turned a business plan into a financial planning practice that grew to become one of the most successful financial planning businesses in the country. It's powerful reading. Erin's ability to convert a practice into a business, one that thrives without her micro-managing, is a skill to be emulated by others."

—**Joby Gruber,** Chief Operating Officer, Aliier Global

"Advisors practices hit the 'ceiling of complexity' at around the $200,000 revenue level with most never breaking through or discovering the highly prized code of a seven figure firm. Erin Botsford, CFP industry rock star & B*arron's* Top 50 Independent Advisor, opens up about what really works to break through that ceiling of complexity, sustain an ideal life, and practice with a seven figure firm."

—**SteVan H. Gates,** CRPC®, Private Wealth Advisor, Allegis Wealth Management

"I seldom enjoy these types of books, but this was a great read! Erin is the Queen of implementation. She has not only created the systems and processes to ensure success, but she's actually applied them in her own practice with outstanding results."

—**Jeffrey A. Concepcion,** ChFC, President & Chief Executive Officer, Stratos Wealth Partners, Ltd.

"I have had the privilege of consulting with hundreds of advisors, including Erin Botsford, regarding practice management strategies throughout my 17 year career in the financial services industry. Erin has created a formula and road map to drive a practice to new levels of productivity and revenue. Her journey as stated in her book has been both compelling and inspiring, one that advisors both new to the business and with years of experience must read. They say, 'Experience is the best teacher,' and Erin's new book delivers."

—**Peter M. Jawidzik,** Managing Partner and Business Consultant, Stratos Wealth Partners, Ltd.

"Erin Botsford has learned and done what it takes to create a dream life as a financial advisor. What an advantage to those aspiring to the same to have access to the wealth of wisdom, encouragement, and sage, actionable advice on all aspects of creating an extraordinary practice that she shares in this book."

—**Dan Sullivan,** Founder of The Strategic Coach, Inc.

"At a time when the financial advisory profession is experiencing a dearth of talent, Erin Botsford shares her personal story describing how she turned headwinds into tailwinds to create a business that has been personally fulfilling, financially rewarding, and impactful on the clients and employees with whom she's worked. This book is an insightful read for anyone considering the business of providing financial advice as a career and is an especially inspiring tale for women considering this profession. Erin is an example of how to conquer the unconscious bias of others and one's own fear of failure. Erin not only touches on the emotion of building a business, but on the practical aspects of executing a plan that takes emotion out of the equation. *Seven Figure Firm* is a worthy read for financial professionals seeking ideas and examples of how to transform from managing business to running a true business enterprise."

—Mark Tibergien, CEO, Pershing Advisor Solutions, a BNY Mellon company

"The best in the business are coachable, curious, and committed to building legacy businesses built for generations of clients and team members. Having coached Erin and her team, their focus on a lifetime of learning, changing and improving, and sharing with others is intentional. Their business is certainly one every advisor can learn from."

—Ray Sclafani, CEO, ClientWise®

"In my two decades in the financial service industry, I've met none better than Erin Botsford. If you are a wholesaler, buy this book for your financial advisors! It's a treasure chest of information."

—Nathan Medin, Senior Partner, Universal Financial Consultants

"If you are looking for the how and not just the why of building a successful practice, this is the book for you. Erin focuses on teaching you her process, and the results will follow. We know how much Erin cares about people and how committed she is to doing meaningful work. The *Seven Figure Firm* approach is clear evidence that Erin's principles drive superior performance."

—Roseann (Ro) Morrison & Chris Dungworth,
Managing Partners, Ro Morrison & Associates

$even

FIGURE

FIRM

$even FIGURE FIRM

How *to* Build *a*

Financial Services Business

that Grows Itself

ERIN BOTSFORD

GREENLEAF
BOOK GROUP PRESS

This publication is designed to provide accurate and authoritative information in regard to the subject matter covered. It is sold with the understanding that the publisher and author are not engaged in rendering legal, accounting, or other professional services. If legal advice or other expert assistance is required, the services of a competent professional should be sought.

Published by Greenleaf Book Group Press
Austin, Texas
www.gbgpress.com

Distributed by Greenleaf Book Group

For ordering information or special discounts for bulk purchases, please contact Greenleaf Book Group at PO Box 91869, Austin, TX 78709, 512.891.6100.

Design and composition by Greenleaf Book Group
Cover design by Greenleaf Book Group
Cover image©iStockphoto.com/Varijanta;
NUMAX3D, 2016. Used under license from Shutterstock.com

Cataloging-in-Publication data is available.

Print ISBN: 978-1-62634-408-2

eBook ISBN: 978-1-62634-409-9

Part of the Tree Neutral® program, which offsets the number of trees consumed in the production and printing of this book by taking proactive steps, such as planting trees in direct proportion to the number of trees used: www.treeneutral.com

TreeNeutral

Printed in the United States of America on acid-free paper

17 18 19 20 21 22   10 9 8 7 6 5 4 3 2 1

First Edition

This book is dedicated to Kevin William Botsford, a true American patriot, a loving husband, a dedicated father, and my one and only child. To say I am proud of the man he has become would be an understatement. The most meaningful moments of my life have been those spent nurturing his character and, more importantly, his soul.

CONTENTS

FOREWORD

Henry David Thoreau famously said, "Go confidently in the direction of your dreams. Live the life you've imagined." Erin Botsford has figured out a strategy to do just that for herself, her family, friends, clients and even orphans in Africa.

She didn't have a guidebook. She has done it on her own by trial and error with dogged determination, hard work, ingenuity, enthusiasm and empathy.

The wonderful thing about Erin is she is sharing her approach with the rest of us, so anyone running a business (and let's face it, we are all running a business called "ourselves") can live the life they've imagined too.

I met Erin several years ago when I interviewed her on *Consuelo Mack WealthTrack,* my national weekly investment program on public television. She had come highly recommended by a close friend and fellow journalist, Mary Beth Franklin who was personally and professionally impressed by Erin's trademarked investment philosophy "Lifestyle Driven Investing™." Her philosophy has since caught on industrywide, because it makes so much sense.

Erin had been named to the Barron's Top 100 Independent Financial Advisors list, as well as its Top 100 Women Financial Advisors. She had also just come out with her first book: *The Big*

Retirement Risk: Running out of Money Before You Run out of Time,
which made the best-seller list.

I read the book and researched Erin and I came away very
impressed by both. We invited her to appear as a guest on *Wealth-
Track*, the first of what would and will be many appearances.

I have always been fascinated by the stories of very successful
people. What motivates them, what did it take to get there and
what could I learn from them to apply in my own life? *Seven
Figure Firm* is an amazing story about a woman who has created an extraordinary life for herself and others, that now extends
to hands-on global philanthropy. It is a page-turner that I didn't
want to put down. I read it pretty much in a single day.

As a pre-teen Erin's family lost everything when her father died
suddenly, leaving them without savings or insurance. The family
suffered another blow when, through no fault of her own, Erin
was involved in a fatal car accident with a motorcyclist at the
age of 16. Both experiences taught her a searing lesson: without
money you have few, if any, choices. At an early age, she resolved
never to be without money again and learn everything she could
about finance and investing. She has done that and so much more.

In *Seven Figure Firm*, Erin tells her remarkable story about
achieving financial security for herself and her family while building a thriving business that she has intentionally designed to
run without her. This strategy enables her to devote more time
to spreading the word about Lifestyle Driven Investing™, visit
with her grandchildren and focus on her philanthropic work.
Erin helps with causes from serving returning military veterans to

providing water wells, orphan homes and other humanitarian aid to women and children in Africa.

Although this book was written for financial advisors, it has been an eye opener for me. It provides excellent advice for other entrepreneurs who want their businesses to grow and last.

Erin is making a huge difference in many lives. *Seven Figure Firm* can help you do the same and live the life you've imagined.

—Consuelo Mack
Anchor and Executive Producer
Consuelo Mack WealthTrack

ACKNOWLEDGMENTS

I would like to thank my husband, Bob Botsford, who has stood by me in all my business endeavors and wild adventures. His steadfast and unwavering belief in me has been the rock upon which I built my business and my life. Not only did he have a successful career as an airline pilot, but also he has been the CFO for our company since the day we started.

I would like to thank my longtime business partner, Kay Lynn Mayhue, who has been integral to the success of our firm. I still remember the day years ago that I came home all fired up from a very inspiring session of Strategic Coach® and announced I was going to go build a large firm. I told Kay Lynn I needed her to run the business while I did that, and I asked if she would be willing. Quite to my surprise, she said, "Yes," and she's done so in a consistently excellent way. I never could have predicted that our efforts would result in such amazing success. To her credit, she has kept the wheels from coming off more times than I would care to admit! When you move as fast as we have over the years, you must have someone like Kay Lynn by your side with a wrench in her hand!

Much gratitude is also owed to my team at the Botsford Group, past and present, who believed in me and helped me create the business we have today. Their efforts allowed us to build a business that runs like a well-oiled machine without my day-to-day involvement. Their unwavering loyalty gave me the peace of mind to explore new business ideas and pursue my charitable endeavors.

I thank God for giving me an amazing family. My son, Kevin, has been a constant source of inspiration to me. His love for country found him in the heat of battle on more than two hundred combat missions in the US Air Force. Never once complaining, he spent many holidays on the battlefield while the rest of us enjoyed our turkeys and Christmas trees. His wife, Kristin, brilliant in her own right, held down the fort and made the sacrifices asked of a military spouse. Not only is she a praying wife, she is also a great mom to my grandsons, Cooper and Carson. No words can describe my love for these two boys, who thrill me with their very being. I pray they grow to be men of God, following in the footsteps of a great legacy of Godly men.

Let me also acknowledge my extended family of McGowans and Botsfords. Your unwavering love and support, often from afar, has been a source of constant encouragement. I am also grateful to my friends who have stood by me through thick and thin and, at times, told me the truth. You have helped me keep balance in my life. Thank you for being my social directors, the source of much laughter, and more importantly, my prayer warriors.

Much gratitude, as well, to Dan Sullivan and Babs Smith, creators and founders of The Strategic Coach Program®, who have played an instrumental role in my business success. There is no way I would be where I am without Strategic Coach. My favorite saying from Dan is, "Always keep your future bigger than your past." I have attempted to live my life true to that motto.

I would be remiss if I didn't also mention Hal Burleson, my first mentor and a good friend. He did so much to help me succeed in my earliest years in the business. I will never forget the way Hal would stop and put his pencil down whenever I had a question for him. His generosity of spirit and his abundance mentality are forever embedded in my soul.

Finally, I want to express my gratitude to our clients who took a chance on me, even when I was a young female in the South. The hardest decision in the world is trusting someone else with your health or your money. I am honored that so many chose to trust me with their finances, their future, and their legacy. It was our clients who helped me challenge traditional assumptions and come up with ideas that eventually became our business model, "Lifestyle Driven Investing.™" Thank you from the bottom of my heart.

INTRODUCTION
Succeed—ME?

I am probably the least likely person ever to have succeeded in the financial services business.

And yet I have. Beyond my *wildest* dreams.

I still recall that July day many years ago when I sat down to meet with my new boss. He was the one who hired me for my first job as a stockbroker. I had just spent three weeks training in the home office, and now I was back in his office, ready to discuss the business plan that would launch me into my new career. I had worked so hard to get the business plan just right and was excited to share it with him.

My boss sat back quietly and listened to my presentation.

When I was done, he said, "Honey, I have to give you a lot of credit. You have come up with an incredible business plan, probably better than most I have seen . . . But I have to tell you up front—this is never going to work. You're a sure recipe for disaster."

I was almost too stunned to speak. I managed to compose myself enough to ask him why he assumed I would fail.

"Because you are young, you are a female, and this is the South. It's never going to work," he said.

He wasn't trying to be mean. After all, he had hired me and was willing to give me a shot. It's just that he couldn't help thinking like the male chauvinist he was. He was very much a product of his times.

Granted, my boss was right about a few things. I was young. I was female. I was in the South.

I had a few other strikes against me too.

I had no connections. My husband was in the US Air Force—he was an F-15 fighter pilot—and because of the requirements of his training, we had moved seventeen times in the first fourteen years we were married. We had recently moved back to the United States, and I knew very few people in my community.

I didn't come from money. My dad died when I was eleven, leaving my family destitute.

I was also a mom. My son was only five years old when I started, and he needed looking after when the school day was done.

But that man wasn't right about me.

I told myself that failure wasn't an option.

There was NO way I was going to fail. That man's words fueled a fire inside my belly.

• • •

Today, I am the founder and CEO of Botsford Financial Group, a boutique planning firm with offices in Dallas, Texas, and Atlanta, Georgia. I am a Barron's Top 100 Independent

Advisor[1] and a Top 100 Women's Financial Advisor. I am known for a trademarked investment philosophy called Lifestyle Driven Investing™. I am invited to give keynote addresses across the country. I am sought after for my ability to teach, train, and motivate other producers. In fact, when I was asked to train the twenty-five top producers of a major insurance broker/dealer, their average production was up over more than twenty-five percent the following year.

I am convinced if someone like me can create this level of success in the financial services industry, then so can you.

But it takes more than drive. And that is why I wrote this book. I want to share the systems, strategies, and mind-set I used that have propelled my business to the top.

Consider this. If you had chosen to become a doctor, lawyer, or CPA, instead of a financial advisor, you would have a clear, defined pathway to professional success. Generally speaking, the people who are drawn to such careers tend to be comfortable fitting into formalized, hierarchical structures. Hence, their willingness to complete the additional years of post secondary education. These are people who tend to be comfortable following the prescribed paths that lead an associate to partner, and a partner to senior partner. Not so for most financial advisors. As my business coach, Dan Sullivan, has pointed out, the barriers to entry are

---

1   *Barron's* ranking of the top 100 financial advisors is based on assets under management, revenue generated for the advisors' firms, and the quality of advisors' practices.

relatively few for financial advisors. Our profession attracts "rugged individualists" with an entrepreneurial nature. And because of our entrepreneurial nature, we tend to be less accepting of structured paths to success. We seem almost fated to reinvent the wheel as we figure out how to achieve career success on our own.

Not so long ago, you could enter the business through just two gates. You could enter through the insurance industry gate or become a stockbroker through the wire house portal. (I entered through the stock-brokerage portal.) After entering through one of these gates, you were given two types of training: sales training and product knowledge training. Once you left the home office and passed all your exams, you were left to sink or swim based on your own ingenuity and internal fortitude.

Now there are more points of entry. Today, for instance, more and more universities are turning out graduates in the field of financial planning. And these graduates seem to be a new breed of financial advisor. They want to move into structures that are akin to those in the big accounting firms, where there are job descriptions, training programs, and pathways to partnership. However, the reality is that they will go to work for "rugged individualists" who expect their new employee to be totally comfortable with on-the-job training. In some cases, they are expected to learn by "osmosis." I can relate. I had to learn much of what I know today the hard way—by trial and error and sheer determination.

Certainly that's a tough road.

Fortunately, there's an easier, surer route to success. Learn from someone who has been in your shoes and has figured out what works and what doesn't. I have to assume, if you're reading this book, that you want to achieve an even higher level of success and that you are ready and willing to learn.

With that in mind, let me begin by sharing three essentials pieces of advice. First, realize that prospecting is forever. *You can never stop prospecting.* I wish I had known that from the beginning. For some reason, I had it in my head that all I had to do was prospect for seven years and new clients would magically find their way to my doorstep from that point forward. I didn't realize my entire career would be dominated by business development activities. I think I would have been okay with that realization; I just didn't know it early on in my career.

Second, *learn to think like a business owner instead of a product salesperson.* I wish someone had made that clear at the start as well. Yes, I had heard vague talk about "building my own business," but it didn't occur to me that a business was an entity that should be able to run on its own, without the day-to-day involvement of its owner. I learned later that if the business relied upon me, it really wasn't a business. Rather, I had just bought myself a job.

The other key is to create systems that facilitate success. When you break it down, there are five keys to success in this business— Marketing, Branding, Leverage, Systems and Processes, and Personal Discipline. I'll talk about each of these keys at length in the chapters ahead. I'll explain how to use each to organize your own financial services business.

There is no doubt in my mind that if you use even a few of my tips to organize your business, then you, too, can succeed beyond your wildest dreams. As I said before, if someone like me can do it, then so can you!

CHAPTER I

FROM BROKE TO
BARRON'S TOP 100

E very time I am asked to give an industry speech, I always make a point of telling my personal story as well as my business story. Why? Because I am quite aware that everyone in the audience is sizing me up. They want to know what advantages I have had that allowed me to become successful. After all, I'm the one at the podium. It's just human nature to wonder what "edge" I had and, what connections were available to me.

What I have learned over the years is that if I don't tell the audience my story, some audience members will make one up about me. And that won't be to my advantage.

MY PERSONAL STORY

What gave me the inner conviction as a young stockbroker to know I could succeed—even when the man who hired me was convinced I would fail?

I knew I could succeed because of what I had already overcome.

Up until the age of eleven, I had a normal life. I was the fifth of six children born to loving, Irish-Catholic parents. We lived a middle-class life in the Midwest. My father, a highly educated man, worked as a psychology professor in the Chicago area.

He had always dreamed of opening a clinic for early childhood education in Southern California. He had visited the San Diego area after World War II and loved everything about California. He truly believed our family could have a better life in Southern California.

Ultimately, he decided to take a leap of faith and go for his dream. He quit his job, borrowed against his teacher's pension, and moved our family to the West Coast. He took a job selling cars so he could earn money while he waited for his California teaching certificate to arrive. Once it arrived, he would be allowed to open his clinic.

It wasn't to be.

Six months after we moved to California, my father collapsed. He died of a massive heart attack on Valentine's Day, in front of my mother, my siblings, and me. He was fifty years old. I was only eleven.

In an instant, our lives changed forever. My father left our family a $10,000 life insurance policy. That was it. He never imagined that he wouldn't be there to provide for the family he cherished. Since he had borrowed against his teacher's pension, there was no pension benefit available for our family. We went from middle class to broke, overnight.

From that day forward, everyone in our family had to work. My mother needed all of us to pull our weight financially just to keep the lights on. I got my first job before I turned twelve. I earned $1 per hour as a babysitter. I was lucky; most of my friends were working for fifty cents an hour! Every dime my siblings and I made had to be turned over to our mother so she could keep a roof over our heads and food on the table. Her only income was her Social Security benefit. She received $88 per month for me and my sister, and a small benefit for herself. That was it. I remember my mother pulling me aside and telling me point blank, "If you ever want to get out of poverty, you are going to have to do it on your own. I can't help you." From a young age, I learned both the power and necessity of a strong work ethic.

We were barely scraping by when tragedy struck again. I was sixteen years old, driving to my first "real" job at McDonald's, when I was involved in a terrible accident with a motorcyclist. The driver of the motorcycle was killed, and I was charged with involuntary manslaughter. My mother and I met with an attorney. She was honest about our family's financial situation.

After hearing our story, the attorney spoke to my mother as if I wasn't even there. "Mrs. McGowan," he said, "this is purely a matter of economics. If your daughter will plead guilty to these charges, I will be happy to enter the plea at no cost to you. Your daughter will get the appropriate sentence prescribed by the State of California. But, if she wants to defend herself, it will cost you a lot of money."

I thought surely Mother would never agree to that.

I was wrong.

My mother took a minute to consider what he had said. Then

the next thing I knew, I heard her thank him and acknowledge we had no other option. She told him I would plead guilty!

I was *horrified*. I begged and pleaded with my mother. That's when she looked at me and said the ten words I will never forget:

"Honey, we have no money; therefore, we have no choice."

That was the day I learned *money buys you choices.*

Fortunately, not long afterward, another option presented itself. My older brother had just begun his real estate career and suggested we take out a second mortgage on our home to pay for my defense. We did so, and with the money from the mortgage, our attorney was able to bring in expert witnesses who proved that the motorcyclist was driving well over the speed limit and that he had hit me, not the other way around.

The judge dropped all charges. At the end of the court proceeding, he said, "Take this little girl home. She's been through enough."

I wish the story ended there, but it didn't. Shortly after the criminal proceeding, the family of the young motorcyclist sued my mother and me for a substantial sum of money. I was shocked when the civil suit papers came in the mail because the man's parents had visited me at our home soon after the accident and personally assured me they would not sue me. They told me not to worry; they knew a lawsuit wouldn't bring back their son. So when the papers came, I figured that a fast-talking lawyer had changed their minds.

My mother was terrified that we would lose the only asset she possessed, our family home. She lived with this fear for many years until the case was finally settled, at the eleventh hour, by our auto insurance company, which had come to my defense.

· · ·

These early experiences taught me a lot about the power of money. I learned that without money as a resource, you were basically helpless and could easily be victimized by the system. I learned that the legal system is a scary place, especially for a sixteen-year-old. No one cared that it was an "accident"; they were looking to assign blame. I learned who my true friends were. It's amazing who you can count on when the chips are down. They are usually few and far between.

After the accident, I became what can only be called a work-aholic. I held several jobs so I could earn enough to pay back my mother and put aside money for college. I realized the only way I was going to get out of poverty was to work hard and get a good education.

I got lucky and received a full scholarship (for all four years) to the University of California, Irvine. I even tried to "rush" a soror-ity but found it so ridiculous. There I was with all these carefree freshman girls who were holding candles and singing songs and next to them, I felt like a forty-five-year-old woman. I had gone through so much. I couldn't relate to any of them.

I ended up quitting the first semester. Much to the dismay of many of my friends' parents, I went home and went to work.

My mother never tried to convince me to stay at UC-Irvine. I had told her I wanted to quit and got no argument from her. In truth, even though my father had a PhD, my mother found no value in education. After all, her highly educated husband had left her destitute. But she did make me enroll in junior college as a full-time student. If I didn't, she would lose her $88 a month Social Security benefit. She made it clear that wasn't an option.

So I went to junior college full time and worked full time. I stocked grocery shelves from 4 a.m. until 11 a.m. and then went to school. Sometimes I worked the graveyard shift, and sometimes I worked double shifts and took classes on the weekends. You name it; I did it.

This, ultimately, is what gave me my edge. Given my circumstances, I had no choice but to adopt a strong work ethic, acquire a strong set of coping skills, and demonstrate the resilience to overcome anything that was thrown in my way. I often tell people I am either like the "Energizer Bunny" or one of those dolls that gets knocked over and bounces right back up.

. . .

One really good thing happened as a result of the car accident—a schoolmate I found attractive finally noticed me.

A few months before the accident, on the first day of algebra class, as roll call was being taken, I noticed a great-looking boy named Bob Botsford sitting at the front of the class. He was the most gorgeous human being I had ever seen. Right then and there, I told my two best friends that one day I was going to marry him! Unfortunately, he didn't notice me whatsoever until the Sunday after my car accident. That day, he opened up our local newspaper and saw my picture and the story of the accident on the front page! He told his parents, "That girl is in my algebra class."

Needless to say, once the accident occurred, my life and my priorities changed. I had to grow up overnight, not willingly but out of necessity. I was no longer the girl on drill team and class council who laughed a lot. I was the talk of the town. Everywhere I went, I heard the whispers of people saying, "There's that girl that killed that boy."

I had no time to think about Bob Botsford or anyone else. I was too busy giving depositions—a process that lasted for years—plus working full time and going to school. Lucky for me, Bob pursued me and we started dating during all this chaos. God love him, he definitely stood by me during some pretty horrible moments.

I had another fortuitous thing happen as well. I got to be a contestant on the *Wheel of Fortune*, and I won (ironically winning by solving the puzzle "Down in the dumps")!

People often ask me, "With everything going on in your life, how did you end up on the *Wheel of Fortune*?" That's an easy answer. When I turned nineteen, Bob had asked me to marry him. The bride's parents are supposed to pay for the wedding. Of course my family had no money to pay for a wedding, so I had to figure out a way to pay for it myself. In the meantime, my friend, Marie, mentioned the *Wheel of Fortune* was doing tryouts for "Brides Week" in Burbank. I went to Burbank, tried out, got on, and won!

Thanks to my winnings, and my diligence at saving most of what I had earned, I had accumulated a nest egg of about $22,000—which was no small sum in 1979.

A few months before I married Bob, I invested $3,000 to buy a townhouse in San Diego County with a friend of mine. I was twenty and he was nineteen. We each invested $3,000 and obtained a mortgage for the rest. We rented it for a total of fourteen years and sold it for a decent profit. I decided through that experience I was probably not cut out to be a landlord. After each tenant moved out or was evicted, we had to re-paint and often re-carpet. It certainly cut into our profits.

Soon after Bob and I married, we entrusted the balance of our savings ($19,000) to a stockbroker, who had convinced us we were being smart by investing our "wealth" for future growth. He put our money in four different investments. In hindsight, none of them were appropriate for us. All four investments went belly-up in a very short period of time, and we lost every cent we had entrusted to him.

I was devastated. While it may not have been much money to our broker, it was everything to us! It represented years and years of hard work and sacrifice. I felt stupid, betrayed, and embarrassed. From that day forward, I made it my mission to learn everything I could about money and investing. I was determined never to let what happened to me happen to anyone I cared about.

That experience taught me some valuable lessons that have helped me in my career as a financial advisor. As a result, I really understand, from the clients' perspective, how scary it must feel to turn your money over to an advisor, often a stranger, and "hope for the best." I know what it feels like to wake up one day and be surprised that all your life savings are gone . . . poof. I think the worst part of the experience was that our broker just shrugged it off. He never apologized, because he really didn't care.

Here is the lesson from this:

Don't touch other peoples' money unless you genuinely care what happens to it.

Obviously, all of these experiences shaped the way I feel about money and investing. They gave me the impetus to find my way to this profession. I was able to see up close what poor financial planning—or worse yet, NO financial planning—can do to a family. I know from firsthand experience how easily I could have landed in jail, despite the fact that I had committed no crime, simply because my family didn't have the money to pay for a lawyer. I often wonder how that scenario would have played out; I shudder to think about it. I also learned that accidents happen in an instant. No one gets in their car thinking they will hurt someone that day. I've learned that without good financial planning, an accident that results in a civil lawsuit can threaten to take away everything you have worked so hard to achieve.

I also learned that life happens. Accidents happen. Stock markets happen. Markets go up. Markets go down. I've experienced so much, and like you, I have dedicated the better part of my life to helping people find their way through the countless minefields that threaten to take away their ability to enjoy the fruits of their labor.

. . .

To be honest, that's the part of this work I find most rewarding. I love seeing how good financial planning can help change lives for the better and help our clients avoid financial ruin. Sure, being on the *Barron's* list and receiving industry accolades too numerous to count has been great, as well, but nothing beats this. Although we never get to use testimonials in our business, it doesn't mean we don't get them. Each time a client writes a note of "thanks," it means more to me than any industry award ever could.

Finally, one of the most important lessons I learned is that clients don't want to work with glitzy salespeople in fancy suits with silk ties who show them canned pitch decks or marketing slicks or Callan charts. They want someone who is real and transparent on a personal level. While clients want you to listen to them, they also want to know your story and hear about struggles you have had to overcome.

Every person alive has had challenges, and the financial advisor who can best relate to those challenges has the advantage. For those of you who have led relatively "charmed lives" with few personal challenges, don't think you have nothing to offer here. The stories don't have to be yours. They can be borrowed. You don't have to have similar things happen to YOU to be able to relate to a client. But you have to have stories about people you know or have worked with to be able to relate. It's in the relating where all the magic occurs. (I will say more about this in chapter 6, where I talk about psychology.)

MY PROFESSIONAL STORY

From age eleven to twenty-two, life was certainly tough for me. I had no idea then that I would end up with a fabulous business that has allowed me to help many people and create a great life for myself and my family. After all I had been through, it was inconceivable to me that life would be anything but difficult and painful; that's all I had ever known.

Fortunately, things did turn around. However, I have to say that nothing has ever come easy for me. I have had to work exceptionally hard for everything I have. And that's why my early circumstances, as tough as they were, were a blessing. They gave me the confidence to know that I can overcome all obstacles.

PRE-FINANCIAL SERVICES INDUSTRY EXPERIENCE

After my husband, Bob, graduated from San Diego State University, he became a US Air Force officer, and we set out on our journey to see the world. The requirements of training to be an F-15 fighter pilot are quite arduous, so as I said earlier, we moved seventeen times in the first fourteen years we were married. It was a wonderful adventure, and I loved every move and every new opportunity, even though it did require me to start over in a new college every time.

During this period I was lucky to get jobs in the real estate area, specifically as a title insurance officer. I also took college classes at night. It took me eleven years and seven colleges, but I finally graduated summa cum laude from the University of Maryland, European division.

My first entrepreneurial adventure started when we were stationed in Bitburg, Germany. There were no job opportunities in Germany for military wives like me, so we had to find jobs on the air base, which were few and far between.

Fortunately, my knowledge of real estate came to my rescue. In fact, I found myself counseling friends who were getting ready to return to the United States. In those days, (1985–1988) everyone returning home wanted to buy a house. So I would sit down with my friends and share ideas on how to go back to the States and use their veteran's benefits to buy a home with no money down. I realized I was somewhat of an expert on that subject.

One day a friend of mine, who noticed I was counseling friends and scribbling down ideas on the back of a cocktail napkin, suggested I go to the base education office and offer to teach a formal class on the subject. Keep in mind, I had never taught anything to anyone, nor did I feel comfortable speaking in public. However, I was bored and thought this might be a good challenge; after all, I certainly knew a lot about the subject matter. So, I went into the office of Morale, Welfare, and Recreation (MWR) and asked if I could teach a real estate class.

The woman who ran the office fired off her very first question: "How much are you going to charge for the class?"

"Oh, I wasn't planning to charge anything," I replied. "I am just a housewife looking for something to do."

And then the woman said something profound:

"Well, if you don't charge anything for the class, no one will come. People value what they pay for."

Aha!

People value what they pay for.

What an amazing lesson and a truism that has stuck with me to this day.

I finally blurted out I would charge $25 per person (mind you, this was going to be for an eight-hour class). I would get to keep $20 per person, and the other $5 went to MWR for advertising, etc.

She was fine with that. She also told me that if I were smart, I would create flyers and get a high school student or an enlisted person to post my flyers in the stairwells of apartments on the base, at the base grocery store, in the community bank, and at any other place frequented by most people on base.

She ended our conversation by telling me she would put my class in the semester catalog. I had so little confidence in myself, I just assumed my class would be put in the catalog somewhere between cake decorating and dog obedience!

I quickly went into action, creating my materials for the class. This was 1986, so there was no such thing as PowerPoint. I typed up my syllabus and notes and copied them to transparencies because I planned to use an overhead projector. Then I set about creating flyers. Wow, before I knew it, I was learning how to market myself! I had never done that before.

To make a long story short, I gave my first real estate seminar on January 25, 1987, to twenty-two people. I had never before had to stand up in front of people and speak in public. I can't say I was terrified; but I did feel a lot of apprehension. My saving grace? I knew my topic cold. I had closed hundreds and hundreds of loans in my career so there was little chance my audience would be able to ask me a question I didn't know how to answer.

That was just the start. In the years that followed, I was invited to speak at many, many military bases throughout central Europe. My classes were a big hit. In fact, the newspaper, *Air Force Times,* did a full-page story on my classes, and I was given the opportunity to appear on Armed Forces Television. I was a TV star!

The entire experience of teaching those classes laid the foundation for what was to come. Each experience in my life somehow prepared me for a future assignment. Hence, I never consider anything "random." It has all been a part of the tapestry of my life.

ENTERING THE FINANCIAL SERVICES PROFESSION

We returned to the United States in October 1988. My first thought was to return to the title insurance business or work in real estate. I was offered a job as a mortgage broker and thought that was where I would end up.

However, the Sunday before I was to begin work, we were in

church when a lady was paged and had to leave the service. I figured she was a doctor or something similar to that. When I found out she was a mortgage broker, I knew I didn't want the job. I did not want to work in a business where I would be at the whims of others to the extent that I would have to leave church on Sunday or work on weekends. I know that sounds superficial, but I was determined to have balance in my work and personal life. After all, I had a husband and a son.

Once I made that decision, I had no idea what I was going to do. Fortunately, a friend of mine told me about her stockbroker, Hal Burleson, and said she thought she could get me an appointment with him. I did not own a business suit or a briefcase, so when the appointment was set I had to borrow a suit and briefcase from a friend.

I met with Hal, and he explained in detail what it was like being a stockbroker. Truthfully, I didn't know a stock from a bond and could barely spell mutual fund, but when he said he could probably get me an interview with the branch manager, I was very excited.

On the day of my first interview to become a stockbroker, I was both excited and apprehensive. I was convinced this man was going to recommend that I become someone's secretary. Instead, he said, "Well, kid, I'm going to give you a chance, and I'm going to hire you!" I couldn't believe it. Someone took me seriously! (Or so I thought at the time . . .)

I started studying for the Series 7 test in March 1989, and passed all my tests and trainings by July 1989.

After spending three weeks training at the home office, I came back and was ready to begin my new career. And that's when I had that fateful meeting I described in the introduction. In case you skipped over the introduction (as I often do), let me recap it here.

That was the day I presented my prospective business plan to my new boss.

I had worked *very* hard on it. I wanted to bowl him over and get my career off to a good start.

He *was* impressed with my business plan: "Honey, I give you a lot of credit. You have come up with an incredible business plan, probably better than most I have seen."

It's what he said next that stopped me in my tracks.

"I have to tell you up front—this is never going to work," he said. "You are a sure recipe for failure." And when I asked him why, he said plainly: "Because you are young, you are a female, and this is the South. It's never going to work."

I don't remember how that meeting ended, but I look back and often think those were the kindest words he could have spoken. That day I determined I was going to make him eat those words. I was not going to fail—ever! The phrase "Failure is not an option" became my mantra. That mantra has probably helped me more than any thought I have ever had.

EARLY CHALLENGES BRING VALUABLE LESSONS

Starting out in Panama City, Florida, in 1989 was not easy. The average per capita income at the time was little more than $9,000 per year, and that was true for military personnel as well. We used to call the area L.A. (Lower Alabama). In addition, I didn't know one person in town outside of my husband, and he only had limited resources to invest (like nothing!) But I was determined, and I worked hard. One clear break came: my friend, Hal Burleson, quickly became my mentor. God love him; he was probably single-handedly responsible for my success, and I have probably never adequately thanked him for that. So, again, Hal, THANK YOU!

Hal had been in business two years longer than me and let me follow him around like a puppy dog. He shared every tool and trick of the trade he had learned thus far. I have to say, Hal operated from an attitude of abundance, which was unusual in those days. Most of the other brokers would lock up their desks and their offices and would never share their ideas or marketing techniques. I was fortunate that Hal shared everything he learned. I was a sponge for everything I could absorb. Hal was using public seminars to build his business, and he was kind enough to let me come be his "assistant" so I could learn his techniques. He even went so far as to let me copy, verbatim, his seminar materials!

Hal believed there was more than enough business to go around, even in a small town like Panama City, so he freely shared what he was doing with me. It was an unbelievable gift. Along with the seminars, Hal and I started working on some other marketing endeavors as a part of the multifaceted marketing "machine" we were working on at the time. (I will discuss marketing in detail in chapter 2.) By the end of my first year in business, Hal came to me and said, "Erin, I have never seen a more determined business person in my entire life—male or female. I can't believe how driven you are." Hal was right; I was driven. As I was to discover later, I was driven by the fear of failure. I knew what poverty looked like, and I knew I was never going back there.

Three Major Lessons I Learned During This Time

- Starvation is a wonderful motivator.

- It is better to operate from an attitude of abundance than an attitude of scarcity; there is enough business to go around for everyone.

- Always err on the side of generosity. Hal would drop whatever he was doing when I entered his doorway. He would put down his pen and focus on my question. He was incredibly generous with his time.

QUESTIONS TO PONDER:

- **What drives you?**

If you can tap into the force that drives you, it can be a huge help. Fear of failure is probably not the healthiest of drivers. Healthier thought patterns might have been better, but I did my best with what I knew at the time. It is better to be honest about what drives you than to pretend your motives lie elsewhere.

- **What is your WHY?**

Why are you willing to do what it takes to be wildly successful in this business? This is a HARD business. You better have a big enough WHY to sustain you. My WHY these days is philanthropy. My husband and I have enough money. Everything I do these days is to improve the lives of others. In particular, we support orphans in Africa, and there will never be enough money to take care of all of them.

- **What are your limiting beliefs?**

We all have a belief system that says we can do X, but not more than X. The sooner you acknowledge you have created a ceiling for yourself, the sooner you can punch through that ceiling and create a new set of beliefs. The only reason you have a ceiling is that you have a limited belief system. If someone told you ultimately you could not fail, what would your ceiling be?

For more information and additional resources, go to www.sevenfigurefirm.com.

CHAPTER 2

PROSPECTING/ MARKETING

Without clients to serve, you have no business. The only way to build a business is to get butts in seats! To do this you have to prospect and/or market. While there are differences between the two words ("prospecting" and "marketing"), the bottom line is you have to identify your target market, locate potential customers in your target market, find ways to attract or get in front of them, and then effectively engage with them and convince them to become your clients. This is the most difficult and the most important part of any business. The extent you can master this area of the business is the extent to which you will be successful and your business will grow.

I find it interesting that new entrants to our profession have little idea as to how they will spend their time. For instance, I frequently speak with young people who have decided to become financial planners. They have chosen this route for admirable reasons: they want to help people, they want to potentially own their own business, and they like the financial world. They *think* they will spend their time doing research on stocks, funds, managers, and strategies. They look forward to designing portfolios for clients and guiding them through the financial planning process. They are usually very idealistic about how they will spend their working hours and daydream about the financial education they will glean along the way.

You can imagine the looks on their faces when I tell them that if they want to be successful in this business, they will be spending very little time doing the things they were expecting to do. At least that's the case if they want to be successful. If that's what they want, they will spend the majority of their time prospecting, marketing, and building relationships.

The same is true for YOU. The degree to which you master the art of prospecting is the degree to which you will be successful in the business. Period. In reality, you have to do all of these things (analysis, research, etc.), but if you haven't done the work to find the clients, there is no reason for any of it.

In my case, I thought I would only have to prospect for seven years. Why seven? I don't know, but for some reason I was convinced that after seven years, business would continue to roll in without doing any more prospecting. Wow, what a shock I had in store for me! Not only was I wrong on that, I was VERY wrong. I suppose there was a time I could have chosen to stay relatively stagnant in terms of the growth of the business, but if a business (any kind of business) isn't growing, it is dying. And there is no way to change that economic formula.

So the *first* Key for Success for any advisor is Prospecting and Marketing. You must be a professional prospector, hunter, or rainmaker—or whatever you choose to call it. Call it what you want, but if you can't master this role, you had better team up with someone who can, because you can never achieve high levels of success without having a regular stream of new prospects coming in the door.

For purposes of our discussion, I define *marketing* as something you do to promote your company and its services. It is usually an outbound activity and often does not require your personal involvement. We often do "marketing campaigns," where we send e-mail blasts to clients, prospects, and centers of influence. We create marketing brochures as leave-behind items. You may use the marketing brochures offered by your home office; you may send newsletters, market updates, etc. All of those are marketing activities.

I think of *prospecting* as activities I do that actually require direct involvement, either by me or other members of my team. I call it hunting or rainmaking and I often say: "I am like a lioness . . . I hunt at night." What I mean by this is that I am out and about in my particular circle of influence on many evenings, attending functions, speaking, networking, etc., mostly for the purpose of "hunting down" new prospects. This *never* feels like work to me because I really do enjoy the people who attend these functions. I am someone who loves people, and I love hearing their stories. I am often accused of being a "junky" for people's stories. That's a positive thing, because people, for the most part, enjoy telling their stories. It's a win-win.

Another reason I make a point of being out and about in the business community is to keep in front of people who could one day need our services. You know the saying: "Out of sight; out of mind." I don't let myself be out of sight for too long. Keep in mind, I never do things I don't want, nor will I work with anyone with whom I don't have a shared set of values. Life is much too short to compromise your standards. And finally, I don't just prospect at night. Over the years, I've done prospecting at all hours of the day, depending upon what makes the most sense. In the next section, I'll explain the kinds of activities I have done that have worked particularly well for me.

METHODS OF PROSPECTING— DON'T GIVE UP

There are many ways of prospecting, and the good news is, *they all work.* All you have to do is commit to several methods that you will do simultaneously and work those methods for at least eighteen months before you give up. You cannot decide to *try something* to see if it will work. It WILL work; you just have to give it sufficient time and effort. Certainly, along the way you want to review what is working the best and what is not working as well as you had hoped and modify your plan accordingly. It is clear you have to be flexible, but the key is to not abandon anything for at least eighteen months. Remember, it normally takes seven or eight "hits" with a prospect before they actually commit to doing business with you. That number is pretty constant; the mistake people make is giving up too soon; well before they have made contact with a prospect those seven or eight times. I would go so far as to say the number of "hits" required is probably even higher these days than it was twenty years ago, mainly due to the current economic environment. Investors have been wounded in the past several years, between the financial meltdown of 2008 and Madoff-type scandals. They're more wary than at any time I have seen in the past. They want to know you have staying power. They want to see you will still be in business eighteen months or two years from now before they will trust you with their money.

Since we are on the subject of prospecting, let's talk about "cold calling." During the three weeks I spent training at the home office, I was forced to cold-call. I hated it so much that I went back to my hotel room each night and cried. (Yes, I seriously cried every night!) However, I finally figured out how to rig the training system and started calling my husband and friends each night during our cold calling sessions. There was NO WAY I was going to build a business doing *that*. I had already determined that if cold calling was the only way to make it in this business then I might as well quit right away. Keep in mind: cold calling is still considered a very effective prospecting method. If it's working for you, God bless you; keep doing it. It just didn't work for me.

NO FRIENDS, FAMILY, OR NEIGHBORS

Second, despite the fact that my trainers taught me to focus my efforts on building a list of all my friends and family members as well as people in my direct circle of influence, I made it my policy to NOT do business with friends, family, or neighbors. Wow! How different is that?

Here were my reasons:

- **One:** I didn't know anyone in town so I didn't have an immediate circle of influence. I knew my husband and a couple of other pilots in his squadron, and they clearly didn't have any money.

- **Two**: I knew I wasn't credible to friends and family. They knew I was new to the business, and I'm sure they wanted me to "practice" on other people. Then, too, *I* knew I was new to the business, and I didn't want to "practice" on my family and friends.

- **Three:** More important than all of this, when I announced that I had a policy where I wouldn't do business with friends, family, or neighbors, they suddenly rallied around me and wanted to help.

You must understand the psychology of this decision. Friends and family *want to help you.* They really do. They just don't want to help you to their perceived detriment! If you don't make this statement overtly, everyone will think you are only visiting or reconnecting with them to get your hands into their back pocket so you can pull out their wallets. That is what they fear and that is what immediately puts a strain on your relationship.

Trust me, eventually I ended up doing business with many, many friends and family members, but it took years before they looked at me and realized I was going to be in the business for a while. They surmised I had probably learned a few things along the way, and then they *came to me*, not the other way around. I never, ever asked a friend or family member for business, but ultimately most of them have come to me and said: "Erin, I know you have a policy for not doing business with friends, family, or neighbors, but I wanted to ask you if you'd make an exception for me." And in every case, I did make that exception, but it was a different dynamic than it would have been had I started out begging them for money. Instead, I did meet with friends, family members, and neighbors and asked them to introduce me to their contacts. Knowing my policy, they bent over backward to help introduce me to potential prospects. It was one of the best decisions I ever made, and I'm not sure why it isn't done more often.

SEMINARS WORKED FOR ME

Ultimately, my primary prospecting method turned out to be giving seminars, but in the beginning, I didn't know that's how it was going to turn out. Looking back, my training in Europe giving real estate seminars to GI's probably prepared me to become a public speaker. It is always hindsight that gives you clarity as to how the journey turns out. When you are in the moment, it takes small leaps of faith and belief in yourself that something is going to work! In the beginning, I didn't know what would work so I felt like I had to try everything and do it simultaneously. I *thought* the idea of giving seminars would be right up my alley, but there were two big problems I faced: What would I say to an audience when I knew very little about my subject matter, and how could I get people to attend?

INITIAL PROSPECTING METHODS

These are the initial methods I decided to use in my multifaceted marketing plan. Keep in mind, I sometimes have strange names for what I did, but if you go with it, you'll get what I mean. I want to go through these methods for people who are just getting started. My preferred method of prospecting now is referral prospecting and hosting various types of client events, but until you have your initial pool of clients, it's virtually impossible to do the latter. (I'll talk more about these two methods of prospecting in later chapters.)

Here are the four methods with which I started:

- "Drive-By Shootings"

- "Out-to-Lunch Bunch"

- Practice Seminars for People Who Were Not Qualified

- Real Seminars

"DRIVE-BY SHOOTINGS"

I know this title is horrible, but I would be disingenuous if I didn't tell you what I called it at the time. My friend/mentor Hal and I decided to challenge each other with this prospecting method. Three mornings a week, we'd leave our houses early and stop by small businesses. The object of the game was to get there between 7:00 a.m. and 8:00 a.m., before the receptionist or gatekeeper got there. It was amazing how many small business owners we were able to meet. We would offer to bring in pizza during lunch and give their employees a financial seminar, which I called "The Money School." The business owner would frequently invite us back for a cup of coffee to discuss the economy, the markets, etc. It was a good way to get to know new people in town, and we generally found small business owners very receptive to our unannounced visits. Unfortunately for us, most of their investment capital was tied up in their businesses, which didn't serve our purposes all that well. In hindsight, these would have been ideal candidates for what I do today—full financial planning to uncover their personal and business risks. Today, I'm sure this is the approach I would take. Back then, I was a new stockbroker, and if the business owner didn't have the ability to write me a check for investment purposes, he or she was not a good candidate for my business. On the other hand, because I needed audiences to practice on, the lunchtime seminars I did for the employees of these small businesses ended up making my efforts very worthwhile.

Deciding to use seminars to build my business was not without risk. Early on, I was very worried that someone in the audience might ask me a question I knew nothing about. This was a huge fear for me and with reason; I didn't have a clue about the financial markets. I decided I might as well practice with, and look foolish in front of, people who were not qualified to be my clients (although back then if they could fog a mirror, they were likely qualified)! That being said, this fear drove me to become a student of the financial markets, a skill set that has served me well.

"OUT-TO-LUNCH BUNCH"

This prospecting method will always be my favorite. In fact, I continue to do it today. As I said, when I first started, I knew no one in town, not one person. I actually figured out a way to work that to my benefit! (See, if you stay with me long enough you will realize I can turn any lemon into lemonade!) Shortly after

I got back from home office training and had my business plan approved by my manager, I made a trip to the local chamber of commerce. The young woman behind the counter was very helpful and very nice. I will call her Jane Wynn. I asked Jane to lunch, and she agreed. We met the next week, and I explained to her that I was new in town and didn't know anyone. I asked her about things like where she got her hair cut and what she and her husband did for fun. In fact, I employed a very important technique I had learned from another friend, Dave Norczyk. The technique is simply: "Compliment and Ask Questions." We all know that people like to talk about themselves, so why not let them? I love people, so it was a great way to learn about them.

I asked Jane all about herself, what she did for fun, where she shopped, etc. I kept the focus entirely on her. If she asked about me, I would answer only the question she asked and then I immediately went back to her. I wanted to know all about her job, how long she'd been there, what she liked best, all very positive stuff. At the end of the lunch (which I bought), I said, "Jane, this has been so much fun for me. If you were me and you wanted to meet all the movers and shakers in Panama City, who would you meet with?" Without giving it any thought, she gave me two or three names and their accompanying phone numbers. I asked if it was okay to say she had referred me.

"Of course," she said.

She had enjoyed our lunch very much, as had I. After all, what was not to like? She got a free lunch and she got to talk about herself for an entire hour, and I got to spend time with a really interesting person and bring a new friend into my life. We both won.

When I got back to the office, I immediately got on the phone and called each of the three people and said, "Joe, I just had lunch with your friend, Jane Wynn, and she said you are someone I need to meet. Could I buy you lunch next week?" In at least ninety percent of the cases, the answer was yes. I then proceeded to write Jane a handwritten note, and here's what I said:

Jane,

It was a pleasure having lunch with you today. Thank you so much for taking time out of your busy schedule to meet with me. I learned so much about you and the city. If I can ever do anything to help you in terms of financial planning, please don't hesitate to give me a call. If you don't mind, I will keep you on my mailing list and make sure you get invited to my upcoming seminars. I think you'd enjoy learning about the financial markets from my point of view.

With warm regards,
Erin

I would include my business card, and her name went on my seminar invite list.

From that point forward, I had lunch meetings just like this several days a week for years and years and years. Each time I walked away with a new friend who had been given the gift of talking about themselves for at least an hour, so they always felt like the conversation was great! I built a very impressive list of people, many of whom eventually became my clients. It was probably the most fun and certainly one of the easiest methods of prospecting. The time we spent was primarily focused on them, and I felt confident they would consider reaching out to me if they needed a second opinion or a new advisor. It turned out to be true; many of those people ended up becoming clients over the years.

PRACTICE SEMINARS

As I mentioned earlier, I had decided to build my business by giving investment seminars, but I had no confidence in my ability to answer questions. I remember Hal reminding me that I probably knew more than ninety-nine percent of the people attending my seminars. But, I needed the practice; I needed to be able to speak fluidly and know my material without stumbling, looking at notes, etc. So I offered to give seminars almost anywhere and to anyone who would listen.

To my surprise, I found that I loved talking to firemen! I went to all the local fire stations and offered to give the firemen my seminar. Think about it: these guys were basically captive audiences. They were on duty for twenty-four hours, and unless the alarm went off, they weren't going anywhere. Besides that, they were amazing cooks! They would prepare lunch as they did each day and then I would give them my investment seminar. I did this for quite a few fire stations throughout Panama City. While very few firemen became clients, I learned plenty. They were all very intelligent and asked very good questions. They also had friends, family members, and neighbors who had money so it worked out well for me. I would put them on my mailing list for my evening seminars, and they would invite their friends. Many of them became good referral sources for me.

Also, one very lucrative opportunity came up when I was given the opportunity to manage a portion of their pension fund. Their fund had very strict criteria on the types of investments it could hold, but I found the perfect opportunity for them. I began trading US government zero coupon bonds when the timing on bonds was perfect for this type of activity. Within the first year, we had made so much money using this strategy in a declining interest rate environment that I was asked to give a report to the board of trustees for the pension fund. The trustees had never seen their fund go up so much in such a short period of time. While I was nervous presenting to the board of trustees, it was quite an honor, and subsequently a number of the trustees became my clients!

I also gave "practice seminars" in front of Sunday school classes, senior citizen groups, etc. You name it; I did it. After all, I was hungry, and as I have said before, starvation is a wonderful motivator.

REAL SEMINARS—HOW TO FILL A ROOM

Within a very short time, I went to my manager and told him I was ready for the big leagues. I wanted to start giving investment seminars, either in the evenings or during the day at public libraries. In my naiveté, I assumed my manager would pay for ads in the local newspaper, and hundreds of people would show up! Boy, was I wrong on all counts.

When I announced my plans, my manager made me this deal: He told me I had to use my own efforts to bring in fifteen confirmed bodies at two seminars a month, without using a newspaper ad. If I was successful in doing that for six months, he would allow me to place an ad in the local newspaper at my own expense. Wow, what a huge disappointment that was for me. It meant I had to convince thirty people a month to show up at one of two events. And I had to confirm they showed up. Because I knew no one in town, it seemed like an insurmountable task.

I went to Hal and whined about my dilemma. He quickly told me the manager had made him the same "deal," and he basically told me to quit whining. Well, he didn't exactly say it that way because Hal was never untoward, but he gently encouraged me to get busy and get the job done. So I did. I made up flyers, had them compliance-approved, and started mailing them out to everyone and anyone on the small list I had compiled. Then I went to the phone book and picked more names. That's really how scientific it was. I was very disciplined about calling each person on the mailing list exactly three days later, asking if they had received my flyer, and inquiring whether they were going to come to my seminar. It turned out that almost none of them had any recollection of receiving my flyer, so I struck up a conversation with them on the phone and just invited them to the seminar. If they didn't commit to the next seminar, I at least got them to be polite and consider coming to a future seminar. I knew I needed to get fifteen people to the next seminar, and I realized there would be a lot of no-shows so I figured I needed to get twenty-five to thirty people to say yes the night before in order to get my fifteen. I would always call all the "yes" people the night before and remind them. The night of the seminar, I would pray. Fortunately, I had many seminars with fifteen people, but not always. Sometimes there were four. Sometimes one. But I put on the same show no matter who attended. It was show time and I needed to perform!

I gave my seminars, and low and behold a certain percentage of attendees agreed to meet with me. Then, a certain number of meetings ended up with the prospects becoming clients. I quickly learned it was a numbers game. The more people who attended, the more who set up meetings, and the more who became clients. It was as simple as that!

Whenever possible, I tried to get the follow-up appointment scheduled the night of the seminar. Then the next day I called all the no-shows and reminded them about the seminar they had missed the night before. They usually displayed some kind of remorse for not showing up, and I would let them know when the next seminar would be and ask them to attend. More often than not, they did. Then I would call all the people who attended, and this was my script: "Hi, this is Erin Botsford, and I'm just calling to say thank you for coming to last night's seminar." And then I shut up. I learned that the next person who spoke "lost." If they spoke next, I seemed to get the appointment. If I got nervous and spoke to break the silence, I got nothing. That was a valuable lesson for me.

The interesting thing about this six-month exercise that was essentially forced upon me by my manager is that I probably learned more in those six months than in any six-month period of my career. As it turns out, my manager was exceptionally smart. He wasn't the ogre I made him out to be. He knew I needed to learn a valuable lesson: how to fill a room on my own, with no ad in the paper. True to his word, after six months, he allowed me to start running an ad in the local newspaper, (at my own expense) but I also continued to invite people just as I had before. I had learned how to fill a room. The interesting part about the ad is that it was expensive and was very unpredictable in terms of results. Sometimes I would get a lot of people from the ad, but most times not. That being said, it seemed more qualified people came as a result of the ad, but considering the fact that my phone prospecting list had been created from the white pages of the telephone book, it's not hard to figure out why the ad people were a little more qualified.

Valuable Lessons I Learned from Giving Seminars

- Don't rely on newspaper or radio ads. Figure out a way to fill a room with other methods. That might be a direct mail campaign or using a telemarketer.

- Giving a seminar is an art. You must first "disturb" the prospects about what they are currently doing. If you don't "disturb" them, there is no incentive for them to change.

- There needs to be a call to action at the end. Most advisors don't do this or if they do, they don't do it well.

- You need to have an assistant or someone there to book appointments for you. You will be glad-handing while the others leave.

- You MUST contact every person who attended within twenty-four hours of the seminar. First call the no-shows early in the morning, and then call the others. Don't leave the office until everyone who attended has been called and asked for an appointment.

- The margin of returns drops off dramatically after forty-eight hours. If you have not scheduled an appointment before then, it's not going to happen.

- The seminar is just the beginning. Advisors often forget the purpose of the seminar and think holding the seminar is the goal. They often present the seminar and are so exhausted by all the work it took to get people to the event that they forget the seminar is just the first step. If they don't do the immediate follow-up, it was all for naught. As a guide:

  ◦ Put forty percent of your effort filling the room.

  ◦ Put ten percent of your effort on the actual presentation.

  ◦ Put fifty percent of your effort on the follow-up.

Truthfully you need to give each of these steps one hundred percent of your effort, but this gives you an idea on the importance of follow-up.

- Give thought to the length of seminar. I have seen advisors buy into seminar programs and offer to teach seminars or classes to the same people on multiple nights or in semester-long continuing education courses. My personal experience tells me a one-time seminar that lasts less than two hours is plenty. I have always said a seminar is purely a "tap dance" for credibility. Generally, the people who attend will decide in the first five to ten minutes whether they are going to do business with you.

- Go where the money is. Since I lived in a town where the average per capita income was $9,000 per year, I decided to find out where the money was and go there. It turned out the only money in town was in the hands of "snowbirds" who came to winter in Panama City. So, I gave daytime seminars at the public library, and I prayed each time for rain! (If it rained, the husbands would not play golf; instead, they would come to my seminars!)

I learned a lot in my first few years, and I credit my early success to the combination of all of these prospecting methods. Each activity fed or helped foster the other. At one point early in my career, I was stopping at six businesses each week, setting up at least three lunches per week, and doing an average of six seminars a month with no assistance. Occasionally, I would get a friend to come with me to help at a seminar, or sometimes I would pay one of the women who worked in the office to be my assistant at night. I didn't have an assistant assigned to me until I had been in the business for almost four years!

HIGH ACTIVITY COUNTS

At some point in my first couple of years, my friend Mack Bland gave me some good advice. Mack was in the real estate business, and he saw how hard I was working. He saw the early mornings at the chamber of commerce meetings. He saw the lunch meetings, the seminars going late into the evening; he saw it all. He encouraged me by saying, "Erin, just keep up your activity level and the business will come." I guess it's sort of like the saying, "Sling enough mud and some of it will stick." In the end, it truly was the massive amount of activity I created that resulted in my being "rookie of the year" for my broker training class. While the average broker opened an average of seven new accounts per month, I averaged twenty-two new accounts each month for the first two years of my career. It didn't come easy, but it came—one account at a time. I say all of the above to encourage you. If I did it, then so can you!

MY CAREER EXPERIENCES ITS FIRST HICCUP—STARTING OVER!

As mentioned earlier, I started my career with a brokerage firm in Panama City, Florida. In my first calendar year, I remember making a whopping total of $14,997. I can tell you I have never worked so hard in my life. The next year I made a little over $40,000, which I considered terrific. By my third year I had reached that magic $100,000 level. From my perspective, I felt like I had hit the "mother lode." I was making more than I had ever imagined! I finally had CPAs and other centers of influence referring business to me. I was working hard and experiencing what I considered great results.

About that time, my husband got out of the military and started working for American Airlines, based out of Dallas. It was time to move . . . again. I can't say I was the happiest spouse making yet another move, but keeping my marriage and family intact was important to me, so I bit the bullet and made the move to Plano, Texas, a suburb of Dallas. I stayed with the same brokerage firm but basically started all over again.

So guess what I did? I went to the chamber of commerce and introduced myself to the woman behind the counter and asked her out to lunch. I started the "Out-to-Lunch Bunch" all over again. I started giving seminars in Plano, beginning with public libraries and then larger venues like hotels. It was a little easier because I knew what to expect. Then again, it was really difficult because I knew what to expect. I was hauling flip charts and materials in and out of my car at all hours of the day and night, sometimes falling into bed late at night, only to start the routine all over again in the morning.

SPEAKING TO CLUBS AND ORGANIZATIONS

In addition to doing seminars, I made myself available as a speaker to local clubs and organizations. I went to the chamber of commerce and got a list of all the clubs and organizations in a twenty-five-mile radius from my office. I made up flyers, had them compliance-approved, and sent them out to the program chair of each organization. I learned a couple of things in doing this:

1. The program chair and all other organizational positions change at some point during the year, usually in May. They rarely update this information until about August. To be

sure you catch someone who is in charge of booking speakers for that organization, you should send the same flyer out about every other month, because chances are, it will either be ignored or forwarded to the appropriate person.

2. At the beginning of the program chair's term, they are scrambling to find speakers; so the closer you can time your solicitation to their new position the better.

3. On the flyer, be sure to highlight that you are "available on short notice." Very frequently the program chair will be faced with the unpleasant reality of a speaker canceling at the last minute. Many have told me they hung on to my flyer because they wanted a backup plan if one of their speakers cancels. It actually worked in my favor a couple of times.

4. Know your audience. Know what the group is all about. I can tell you from personal experience how embarrassing it can be to speak on a topic that is controversial to the tenets of that particular club. To illustrate this point, I was invited last minute to a club called the Exchange Club. I had NO idea what they stood for. About five minutes before I was to speak, I asked my host what the Exchange Club was all about, and he told me they believed in "buying American." You have no idea how far my face dropped because my topic and all my props were about "global investing." In about five minutes, I figured out a way to turn my topic into something palatable to this group, but my terror could have been alleviated by having done a little bit of homework. This was in an era long before Google searches and Internet access, so I will cut myself some slack!

5. Have multiple topics you can speak about. This was a huge lesson given to me by my initial manager that worked throughout my career. Most organizations want you to talk for twenty or thirty minutes. I used ten, three-by-five cards and came up with a variety of topics that I could talk on for about ten minutes. Then, depending upon the makeup of the group and the time allotted to me, I could pick and choose topics that might be appropriate for my audience.

Valuable Prospecting/Marketing Lessons

- Your Clients Will Come from the Pool You Swim In

As a rookie broker, I felt very uncomfortable prospecting for wealthy clients. I tended to prospect on the east side of Panama City, which was home to predominantly military people. I felt more comfortable in this circle because I was one of them. On the other hand, most of them, like me, had limited resources and certainly not mega dollars to invest with me. Somehow I had this delusion that even though I was prospecting to military people on the east side of town, by some magic trick the people who would show up at my seminars and/or become clients would be wealthy people from the west side of town.

One of the more successful brokers, Augie Yankee, took me aside and taught me a great lesson. Without being rude or conde-scending, he said these words, "Erin, something I have noticed in the course of my career is that when I prospect on the east side of town, my clients generally come from the east side of town, but when I spend my time prospecting on the west side of town, that's where the bulk of my clients come from." He was pointing out the obvious: All the rich people lived on the west side of town, yet he noticed I was spending the bulk of my time prospecting on the east side of town. I had to admit he was right. I was prospecting poor people and wondered why I had no rich . . . go figure!

- If You're Not on the Phone or You're Not in Front of a Prospect or Client, You're Not Making Money

Another lesson I learned early on came from one of my instructors from broker training, Marlyn Van Meter. She said, "If you're not on the phone or in front of someone, you are not making money."

Over the years, I saw so many brokers deluding themselves by doing activities that would not result in revenue. The most notorious activity that I saw was brokers spending hours upon hours reading *The Wall Street Journal* from cover to cover or working on their Quotrons (that's what we had prior to computers).

Their excuse was that they wanted to be ready to answer questions from people who called them. The sad truth was that if they continued in this behavior and didn't do some form of prospecting, there wouldn't be anyone calling them so the information they were picking up was irrelevant. We all need to know what is going on in the financial markets, but I suggest you do your reading before or after normal business hours.

- All methods of prospecting work if you stick with it.

The key is to constantly refine and fine-tune your strategies, based on your results. One of the biggest mistakes I have witnessed is not the prospecting system used, but the lack of dogged consistency and commitment to using and working the system.

- Immediate follow-up to a meeting or encounter of any kind is paramount.

For instance, if you meet someone at lunch at a restaurant, try to follow up with that person by sending an e-mail from your car while you sit in the parking lot. If they have come to your office, it is impressive if you follow up immediately so they have an e-mail from you by the time they return to their office.

- There is nothing that will ever replace the power of a handwritten note.

Even if you have followed up by sending an e-mail, if you really want to get their attention, follow that up with a handwritten note, addressed by you and stamped with a real stamp. That form of communication is becoming priceless.

QUESTIONS TO PONDER:

- **What kind of prospecting appeals to you?**

If you knew you would have guaranteed success using any of the prospecting methods I mentioned, which type of prospecting method would you gravitate toward?

- **Are you consistent in your prospecting efforts?**

You cannot be "nilly willy" in your prospecting activities. You must be consistent and disciplined, realizing any marketing or prospecting activity you do today may not pay off for eighteen months to two years. As much as anything the spoils go to the one who can hang in there long enough to see their efforts rewarded. While each prospecting or marketing activity needs to be evaluated and tweaked, don't just "try" something and quit after three or four months. I don't know of any activity that pays off in that short a time. I have people who come to me today who saw me speak seven, ten, even twenty years ago! Make an impression, and when the timing is right for the prospect they will seek you out.

- **Do you need to become a better public speaker?**

Public speaking is considered a very scary thing; many people fear it. I have seen financial advisors invite wholesalers to do their public speaking for them. The advisor just fills the room with prospects. Have you ever considered when the speaker walks off the stage, he takes his credibility with him? If you hate public speaking and think that solves your problem, think again. I would consider getting training or coaching to overcome the fear of public speaking, instead, especially if seminars are part of your marketing strategy. Keep the credibility; don't let it walk out the door. That being said, once the prospect becomes a client, there is nothing wrong with having outside speakers present various topics. Just make sure that you are the one introducing them, welcoming your clients, and closing out the event.

For more information and additional resources, go to www.sevenfigurefirm.com.

CHAPTER 3

CREATING YOUR BRAND

I f you want your financial services business to grow, flourish, and withstand the test of time, you MUST find ways to stand out from the crowd. Differentiate yourself from your competitors by creating a unique tool or unique value proposition—or both— to deliver to your clients. If you are not sure how to do this, I will provide examples in this chapter and explain the psychology behind each.

Don't consider this a one-time exercise, however. Make sure that whatever you use to differentiate your business today continues to evolve over time. Everything connected to your brand must be updated regularly so it stays relevant. Be sure to freshen *every-thing*—from your logos to your website to your pocket folders to the pens you give your clients at meetings—at least every three years. (Consider how frequently design trends change; you don't want your materials to look outdated.) The good news is that few advisors do this part well, so if you spend some time on this, you can significantly stand out from the crowd.

DIFFERENTIATION IS ESSENTIAL

From day one, I realized I needed a way to set myself apart from all my competitors. In fact, I had extra incentive to come up with creative ways to impress my prospects and clients because I wasn't going to give my first boss the satisfaction of seeing me fail.

Fortunately, I made a very important discovery while working through my first set of cold calls. As I listened to the individuals on the other end of the line, it occurred to me that the vast majority of prospects already had at least one relationship with someone else in the industry. The question was (and it is the same today), "how could I distinguish myself so prospects know that I have something unique and noteworthy to offer?" How could I pique their interest?

I started noticing that my competitors always used pie chart asset allocations, as if it were a tool required by the regulators. Since I had started as a stockbroker, investments and asset allocations were about the only thing we addressed on a daily basis. My first question to myself was, "How can I jazz up this boring pie chart?" My second question to myself was, "Could I accurately show a person's recommended asset allocation without using a pie chart?"

About the same time, I heard a saying, "In the absence of differentiation, you become irrelevant." Those words always seemed to float across my mind so I decided to create something different from the traditional pie chart asset allocation models. That's how I came up with what I called the **GRID™ Form of Asset Allocation**.

The timing on this was probably a little bit before Morningstar's nine-box grid became popular. In fact, I'm sure I had never seen Morningstar's grid when I created my **GRID**™, or I would have probably used theirs! It's important to also note the context of that time. When I started in the business (in the late 80s), there was no such thing as the Internet. Morningstar rankings came in very large black notebooks with thin papers for each mutual fund ranking. These sheets were updated every quarter. Since subscriptions to Morningstar were relatively very expensive, not all firms bought the subscription, and even those that did, didn't necessarily supply that information to all their local offices. Back then, *we* were the keepers and protectors of all information concerning stocks, bonds, and mutual funds; that was the fun part of the business. Until the Internet came around, we had way more access to information than our clients did. Once the Internet came into existence, it seemed our clients sometimes had access to more information than we did!

The first **GRID**™ I created only had four boxes (see image 3.1). I initially named the boxes "Large Cap," "Mid Cap," "Small Cap" and "Bonds." Sometimes my Grid was labeled "Stocks," "Bonds," "Real Estate," and "Cash." The labels I used depended upon what I was trying to demonstrate to the client. What I noticed from a psychological standpoint was the more buckets there were on the piece of paper, the more inclined people were to write bigger checks. So, if you had one bucket, you would get X amount of dollars. If you had two buckets, you'd get twice as much. If you had four buckets, then you'd get four times as much! I have to assume the client reasoned that it was safer to diversify his or her assets into as many buckets as possible!

Original **GRID**™ Asset Allocation

Large Cap Stocks		Mid Cap Stocks	
Total Value	**$0**	**Total Value**	**$0**
% of Portfolio		% of Portfolio	
Small Cap Stocks		Bonds/Fixed Income	
Total Value	**$0**	**Total Value**	**$0**
% of Portfolio		% of Portfolio	

or

Stocks		Bonds	
Total Value	**$0**	**Total Value**	**$0**
% of Portfolio		% of Portfolio	
Real Estate		Cash	
Total Value	**$0**	**Total Value**	**$0**
% of Portfolio		% of Portfolio	

*Image 3.1: Original Forms of the **GRID**™ Asset Allocation*

At first, I started with four buckets and experimented with which asset classes to include. Then I got a little more serious about creating a viable alternative to pie charts. In my study of the markets, I determined back then that there was a minimum of eight asset classes that should be considered in a balanced portfolio. Hence, my second version of the **GRID**™ contained two quadrants with four asset classes in each (Image 3.2).

Botsford Financial Group's **GRID**™ Asset Allocation

DOMESTIC POSITIONS: INTERNATIONAL POSITIONS:

Large Cap Stocks/ Growth & Income	Mid Cap/Growth	Large Cap Stocks/ Growth & Income	Mid Cap/Growth
Total Value $0 % of Portfolio	Total Value $0 % of Portfolio	Total Value $0 % of Portfolio	Total Value $0 % of Portfolio
Aggressive Growth/ Smallcap/Sector	Cash/Bonds/Fixed Income	Aggressive Growth/ Smallcap/Sector	Emerging Markets
Total Value $0 % of Portfolio	Total Value $0 % of Portfolio	Total Value $0 % of Portfolio	Total Value $0 % of Portfolio

Image 3.2: Second Iteration of the **GRID**™ *Asset Allocation*

On the left-hand side, the grid allocated space for all their domestic positions, and on the right-hand side, it allocated space for all their international positions. Looking at image 3.2, on the upper left, you will see the categories I used: "Large cap"; "mid cap"; "small cap"; plus "cash, bonds, and fixed income." On the right-hand side, the grid allocated space for their international positions. The international categories I used were "large cap," "midcap," "small cap," and "emerging markets."

My **GRID**™ form of asset allocation has been proven to be invaluable. It shows at a glance how different my firm's approach is from our competitors' approach. We have made sure to update it regularly, so the grid has evolved many times over the years. It looks far different today than when I first started.

THE PROBLEM WITH PIE CHARTS

Let me explain why my **GRID**™ form of asset allocation is much better than a pie chart. Have you ever seen a pie chart asset allocation that reminds you of Pac-Man?

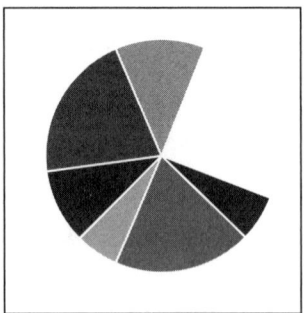

Image 3.3: Traditional pie charts fail to indicate what asset classes have been excluded—intentionally or unintentionally

Of course not! A pie chart must add up to one hundred percent or it looks like an incomplete asset allocation. But a pie chart does not show clients what they don't have or what has been left out of the recommendation. It is, by its nature, an incomplete picture. And yet, I have found that 99.9 percent of the time, my competitors would come to the table armed with a pie chart.

With the **GRID**™, you have predetermined categories that should be considered in every portfolio. That doesn't mean every asset class will or should be selected, but it should be considered. Perhaps a particular client does not want any exposure to emerging markets. Then that quadrant would have a ZERO in it. That's fine. The point is, we considered the asset class and we chose not to include it. It very easily shows up as a missing category because it has a ZERO in the column. Pie charts have no zeros, so they have no way of demonstrating what is missing.

Here's a real example of how I used my **GRID**™ to win a client. In the mid-1990s, I had a prospect—a Delta airline pilot who had recently retired. He had several million dollars to invest. He came to me and said, "Erin, I want to see, based on my goals and objectives, what you would do using $1 million, as an example. What I'm going to do is get a proposal from one other advisor whom I've been talking to, and I'm going to show you his proposal and show him your proposal." I thought it was interesting that he told me that, because the truth is most prospects do visit with multiple advisors, probably more so than they did twenty-five years ago.

It was the first time in my career someone was actually honest about that with me so I said, "Fair enough," and agreed to the challenge. I told him I would like to see my competitor's proposal first. He said, "That's fine." I could have bet and won a lot of money, simply by predicting the kind of asset allocation model my competitor would propose. Of course it was a pie chart! All I did was take my competitor's pie chart and plot what he was proposing on my grid.

His proposal recommended allocating that $1 million in the following way:

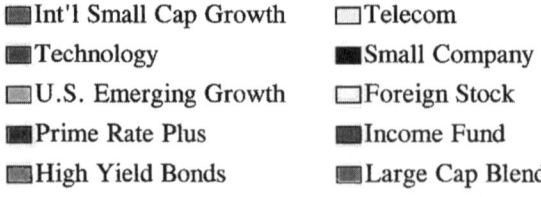

Image 3.4: Competitor's Investment Proposal as it came in a Pie Chart Asset Allocation

THE COMPETITOR'S PROPOSAL VS THE WINNING PROPOSAL

This case ended up being very easy to win. All I did was convert the numbers/percentages that showed up on my competitor's pie chart to my **GRID**™ form of asset allocation (see image 3.5). I won that client because I was able to clearly demonstrate that my competitor had completely discounted or left out a number

Competitor's Proposal on "The GRID™"
Proposed Asset Allocation: $1,000,000

DOMESTIC POSITIONS: $680,000 68.0%		INTERNATIONAL POSITIONS: $320,000 32.0%	
Large Cap Stocks/ Growth & Income	**Mid Cap/Growth**	**Large Cap Stocks/ Growth & Income**	**Mid Cap/Growth**
0	Mid Cap Value $140,000	Int'l Growth $140,000	0
Total Value $ - % of Portfolio 0.0%	Total Value $140, 000 % of Portfolio 14.0%	Total Value $140, 000 % of Portfolio 14.0%	Total Value $ - % of Portfolio 0.0%
Aggressive Growth/ Smallcap/Sector	**Cash/Bonds/Fixed Income**	**Aggressive Growth/ Smallcap/Sector**	**Emerging Markets**
Emerging Growth $100,000 Small Growth $80,000	Prime Plus $120,000 Income Fund $130,000 High Income Bond $110,000	Global Tech $80,000 Global Telecom $50,000 Global Small Co $50,000	0
Total Value $180,000 % of Portfolio 18.0%	Total Value $360,000 % of Portfolio 36.0%	Total Value $180,000 % of Portfolio 18.0%	Total Value $ - % of Portfolio 0.0%

*Image 3.5: Competitor's Proposal on Our **GRID**™*

of asset classes. More importantly, because my competitor had used a pie chart, the prospect had no way to know which asset classes had been left out. You will then see what I proposed (see image 3.6). Since I could always count on the competition to use a pie chart, my **GRID**™ form of asset allocation made it relatively easy to differentiate myself from the competition. It's proven itself to be one of the best differentiation tools I have created.

Botsford Financial Group's Proposal
Proposed Asset Allocation: $1,000,000

DOMESTIC POSITIONS: $800,000   80.0%

Large Cap Stocks/ Growth & Income		Mid Cap/Growth	
Large Growth	$200,000	Mid Cap Growth	$100,000
Large Value	$100,000	Mid Cap Value	$100,000
Total Value $300,000		**Total Value** $200,000	
% of Portfolio 30.0%		% of Portfolio 20.0%	

Aggressive Growth/ Smallcap/Sector		Cash/Bonds/ Fixed Income	
Small Growth	$40,000	Prime Plus	$100,000
Samll Value	$40,000	Income Fund	$50,000
Sector	$20,000	High Income Bond	$50,000
Total Value $100,000		**Total Value** $200,000	
% of Portfolio 10.0%		% of Portfolio 20.0%	

INTERNATIONAL POSITIONS: $200,000   20.0%

Large Cap Stocks/ Growth & Income		Mid Cap/Growth	
Int'l Large Growth	$50,000	Int'l Mid Growth	$25,000
Int'l Large Value	$50,000	Int'l Mid Value	$25,000
Total Value $100,000		**Total Value** $50,000	
% of Portfolio 10.0%		% of Portfolio 5.0%	

Aggressive Growth/ Smallcap/Sector		Emerging Markets	
Int'l Smallcap	$25,000	Emerging Markets	$25,000
Total Value $25,000		**Total Value** $25,000	
% of Portfolio 2.5%		% of Portfolio 2.5%	

*Image 3.6: Botsford Financial Group's Winning Proposal on the **GRID**™*

BLOCKS PLAN—A GREAT WAY TO OVERCOME HIDDEN EMOTIONAL BARRIERS TO MOVING FORWARD!

Another unique tool we created is something we called our "Blocks Plan." Back in 1995–96, I started working with the senior executives of a major Fortune 500 company. In 1999, the company went public and ended up tripling the value of its company stock. The employee who thought he would retire with $3 million in stock now had $9 million. The guy who thought he would have $5 million now had $15 million.

While working with more than 150 of these executives, we discovered most of them had never done much in the way of comprehensive financial planning. In fact, many of them had ninety percent of their net worth in this single publicly traded stock. Their other largest asset was typically their personal residence.

As you might imagine, these executives were extremely loyal to their employer and their stock. You could even go so far as to say they felt an emotional attachment to the stock. Therefore, they were exceptionally reluctant to sell large portions of their stock all at once, even though they knew it was the smartest move financially. Emotion had clouded their thinking. It didn't seem to matter that this was during the dot-com era and companies like Enron, MCI WorldCom, and Sprint had their stock prices fall dramatically, some even to zero. It didn't seem to matter that dozens of companies had gone completely out of existence. They weren't looking at this through the lens of logic. From an emotional standpoint, they just weren't ready to part with company stock.

This was understandable. Some had worked for the company for thirty-five years. The company had not only paid them twice a month for those thirty-five years, it had also given them stock, and now the stock had made them rich.

The IPO for this company was very popular, so there was a lot of competition in the marketplace for these clients from other advisors. We started seeing proposals from our competitors recommending that clients sell fifty to seventy-five percent of their company stock immediately after the IPO and reposition the proceeds into managed money or mutual funds. No one could argue with the viability of those proposals, but there was no way these clients were going to do that. Their loyalty to the company was just too strong.

I was concerned because I held myself out as a certified financial planner. With that designation came a fiduciary responsibility to do the right thing and give the right advice. Everyone knows holding ninety percent of your net worth in a single publicly traded stock is not the right thing to do. At first, however, we were no more persuasive than our competitors in convincing these executives to sell large portions of their stock.

One morning, I went for a long run, and the solution came to me. I created the "Blocks Plan." It was a very strategic way to get around the resistance we had repeatedly encountered when we recommended that executives sell $5 million of their stock right now. Rather than fight that losing battle, we created a plan that would sell tranches (portions) of stock at predefined price points. We called the tranches "blocks."

We would say, "Mr. Client, your stock is trading at $70 a share.

To meet your retirement income needs, we have calculated you will need to reposition $5 million of your stock. You can sell all $5 million now or we can sell in blocks, such as $1 million worth of stock at $70 a share, $1 million worth when it hits $72.50, $1 million worth at $75, $1 million worth at $77.50 and $1 million worth at $80 per share. Can you agree that, if and when it hits these price points, it would make sense to sell these amounts?" That was a much more palatable suggestion or recommendation than to sell $5 million today.

Usually we separated the stock positions into five blocks. Sometimes, if the price went up quickly, we might sell three blocks at one time because those target prices had been reached.

In addition, we had a plan to sell a certain amount if the stock started declining in value. They essentially agreed to a drop-dead price point. If it fell to that point, they agreed to sell all $5 million. They were convinced the stock price would never fall, so getting them to agree to a drop-dead price was really not an issue. That being said, we certainly didn't want to risk another Sprint or WorldCom situation, where some of their employees rode the stocks all the way down to the bottom.

The Blocks Plan actually worked out very well. In fact, we soon realized we had coined a term. Not only did our clients use this term, but we found out our competitors referred to their shares as blocks as well. The word itself helped those executives gain a measure of detachment. We were no longer referring to the stock as "stock," but "blocks," which seemed much more palatable to the client. It proved to be very successful at helping clients do something they knew they needed to do but weren't comfortable doing.

YOUR RULES—YOUR BRAND

I have been in this business for almost three decades. One thing that has kept it fun and "fresh" for me is changing things up when there is a good reason to do so. A business has to evolve if it is to thrive over the long term. One time my coach, Dan Sullivan, said, "You get to set the rules for the people you are going to work with, and you're allowed to change those rules."

In the decades I've been in business, I've changed the rules of my practice many, many times. I tend to draw a proverbial line in the sand and say, "From now on, these are the new rules of my business and this is how I'm going to work going forward." I lay out the rules to the next potential client, and if they accept the terms of my business proposition, they are allowed to become a client. If they don't agree to those terms, they are not a good fit for our business.

When I first started in the business, I wasn't really aware that I needed to have rules or set boundaries for my business—what I would or would not do, how much I would charge, whom I would accept as a client, etc. Early in my career I basically took anyone who could fog a mirror as a client and jumped through hoops for them day or night. As time went on, I realized this was no way to run a business. However, back then there were very few people who trained, mentored, or coached people like me on business or practice management.

Yes, there were seminars offered by wholesalers, and these wholesalers said we needed to create account minimums. So I created account minimums. There was definitely a movement encouraging a shift from commission-based business to a new model in which advisors charged a percentage for assets under management. Even under that model, however, most of us did a lot of work for free. We did research, typed up proposals, and presented our ideas only to see our ideas go down the street to Schwab.

With the advance of the Internet and a raging bull market in the late 1990s, many individual investors were convinced they could invest all on their own. We started seeing clients come in for free advice and taking their business elsewhere. Even the results from my seminars started to wane. The people attending seminars in the mid to late 1990s became "tire-kickers." They came to eat the free cookies and get free advice, but my closing ratio following those seminars really went down. It was quite depressing. What was more depressing was that I was doing a lot of work, meeting with prospects, typing up proposals, and sharing my ideas, but to no avail.

I began to feel resentful that the financial services industry allowed this culture to emerge over time. No one expected their attorney or CPA to work for free. I consoled myself by thinking about my realtor friends who also spent a lot of money on gas and a lot of time showing people property, with no guarantee that they would get the sale.

Finally, in 1997, I received mentoring from a woman named Amy Leavitt, and things changed dramatically for me. Under her tutelage, I learned the value of charging a financial planning fee and an annual renewal fee, which is how my business would be positioned thereafter. I am not talking about charging an "assets under management" fee. This is a fee for creating an investment plan or a comprehensive financial plan.

Before 1997, no client had ever paid me a fee to create a financial plan. I decided to draw a line in the sand and said, "I'm not going to change the rules on the existing people who work with me because that's not fair, but I am going to set up a new set of rules for everybody that comes in from this day forward." So from January 1997 going forward, I said I would only take clients who would pay me a financial planning fee.

What I've found is that when you tell your clients what your rules are up front, they either accept them or they don't. For instance, in one of my many rules changes, we decided to charge a financial planning fee and require that the entire fee be paid up front. I also told clients that each year we would charge a renewal fee going forward. The interesting thing is that the clients are always okay with your rules. Planners are the ones who generally have an issue with creating and articulating their own rules. So each year from that point forward, we have sent an invoice, and they have sent a check. There has been no pushback, because we set the stage and the rules up front.

My first financial planning fee was only $250. My minimum planning fee is now $7,500 paid in advance. We frequently charge many multiples of that minimum fee based on the client and the complexity of the case. I only point that out so you can see the evolution of our practice. Every incremental increase in our planning fee was technically a change in the rules. I actually like changing the rules. It means I am making progress and am more in charge of my world and my outcome.

Remember, at one point, the clients got me and all my advice for free! Then I started charging them a $250 planning fee, but they still got me. Fast-forward about two decades and now they are charged $7,500 or more, and they don't get me for every meeting; they get the even more brilliant people on my team!! So you see, there have been many changes along the way. The key is to never be afraid to draw a new line in the sand. It's healthy for you and for your business. Typically, I like to change my rules on January 1 of each year. It tends to coincide with my New Year's resolutions.

LIFESTYLE DRIVEN INVESTING™

My signature piece of intellectual property—the one that allowed me to become a best-selling author—is the trademarked concept, "Lifestyle Driven Investing™." Clearly described in my book, *The Big Retirement Risk: Running out of Money before You Run out of Time,* Lifestyle Driven Investing™ is simple, yet profound.

It was proven to work in the last two market meltdowns (the dot-com bubble and the 2008 financial collapse), which is why I decided to write a book about it. The premise is this: To fund a client's Preferred Lifestyle™, you should first segregate their retirement expenses into various categories. We call the categories "Needs," "Wants," "Likes," and "Wishes." Once their expenses are categorized, our process is as follows:

- Fund their **Needs** with what we call "Lifestyle" investments. The category is merely a filter for evaluating any type of investment. In order to be considered a Lifestyle investment, it must produce an income, either now or in the future. That income MUST BE **safe** or **predictable** or **guaranteed**. If none of those descriptors fit, it is not a Lifestyle investment.

- Fund their **Wants** with what we call "hybrid" investments. Again, there is no such thing as a hybrid investment. The name is a filter through which we evaluate the attributes of an investment we are considering. To be considered a hybrid, the investment must produce an income. But, in this case we could likely never say the income was safe or predictable or guaranteed.

- Fund their **Likes** and **Wishes** with "non-Lifestyle" investments. Non-Lifestyle investments are the broadest category. They would include all the traditional investment products, such as stocks, bonds, mutual funds, ETFs, hedge funds, private equity, and managed futures. Anything tied to a market that can move would be considered a non-Lifestyle investment. Other private investments, like real estate, oil wells, venture capital, etc., would all be non-Lifestyle investments. When our clients have all their needs and wants funded, we encourage them to be as aggressive as they want to be with the rest of their money. Since none of it is earmarked for their ongoing lifestyle needs, they can use these dollars for capital appreciation opportunities they would likely never have considered if they had been doing traditional investing by using Modern Portfolio Theory or systematic withdrawals from a balanced portfolio. Again, the entire strategy is well documented in my book. I hope you will take the time to read it.

I will admit I was very honored when Dr. Wade Pfau, professor at the American College, referenced my concept of "Lifestyle

Driven Investing" as a second school of thought, falling under what he calls the "safety first" approach. Dr. Pfau has been teaching financial advisors all across the country, so I am hopeful Lifestyle Driven Investing™ will catch on. It has certainly served my client base well.

THE BIG RETIREMENT RISK: RUNNING OF MONEY BEFORE YOU RUN OUT OF TIME

While I am on the subject of smart ways to set yourself apart from your competitors, let me tell you how powerful it can be to write your own book. I'll be honest—writing my first book was the most difficult and expensive exercise I have ever undertaken. However, it was also the most fulfilling project and the single best tool I could have created to help leverage our business. I credit the book with catapulting our business to a level I had always dreamed about.

Imagine walking in the front door of your office and seeing a total stranger sitting there, waiting to meet with one of your advisors. They did not come to a seminar; they did not request to meet with you. Or imagine you are on a local TV show as a guest and someone calls in wanting to work with your firm, based on having seen you on TV and then having bought your book. That's when you know you have truly arrived. That's what my first book did for my business.

Once people read the book and agree with our firm's philosophy of money, they are much more likely to be willing to meet with one of my advisors. The book became the ultimate tool for leveraging my business. There are some very big pluses in being a published author:

- It gives you immediate credibility.

- It opens doors to other types of media opportunities, such as radio, TV, and magazine articles. In fact, I was asked (and agreed) to be the celebrity guest on a ten-day Mediterranean cruise shortly after the book came out! We sent out one e-mail and ended up having forty-six clients and friends join us on the cruise.

- It creates amazing leverage. Now when people read my book and understand my philosophy about money, they "get us" and have no issue meeting with one of my advisors rather than with me. In the years since the book was published, I have met with very few of the actual prospects who have since become clients.

- It more than pays for itself. As I said earlier, completing the book cost me a considerable amount of time and money. It was a big investment. That said, the book has paid for itself in more than monetary ways and given me more freedom than I had ever imagined.

We have created many more proprietary tools over the past two decades—some that we still use and some that we shelved. The key is continuing to create and bring about innovations in your business. Most advisors are not very good at this, so it's really not hard to stand out from your competition. Most advisors tend to use their home office marketing material and collateral pieces, which end up looking like everyone else's. It takes a little more effort to differentiate yourself from the rest of the pack, but I can tell you it pays off in spades.

QUESTIONS TO PONDER:

- **What is YOUR unique method or unique value proposition?**

  You MUST find ways to stand out from the crowd. Differentiate yourself from your competitors by creating a unique tool or unique value proposition—or both—to deliver to your clients.

- **Do you have a different way of demonstrating things to your clients or prospects?**

  Is there a way you could distinguish yourself so prospects know that you have something unique and noteworthy to offer? How could you pique their interest?

- **What sets you apart from your competitors?**

  Consider your products, terminology, salesmanship, or presentation style. Are there areas where you're unique? Is there a chance for you to take something tried and true and make it new and singular for your clients?

- **People value what they pay for: Are you working for free?**

  Is it time to review your brand, rules, processes, and pricing structures? If you don't value your talents and skills, then nobody else will either.

  For more information and additional resources, go to www.sevenfigurefirm.com

CHAPTER 4

BUILDING A TEAM

As I said in an earlier chapter, I spent my first three years in the business with a brokerage firm in Panama City, Florida. I built my income to the point where I was bringing in six figures—and then my husband made a career change and we had to move to Dallas, Texas. Although I wasn't happy about that, I did get a big break about six months after we moved to Texas. I was offered the opportunity to give a seminar to nine hundred people who were all offered early retirement packages at a large electronics company. This opportunity marked a turning point in my career.

I was more than ready. I had done enough seminars over the years, for crowds small and large, to be entirely comfortable speaking to a crowd of that size. What I didn't have, however, was the staff support to capitalize on such a great opportunity.

This was back in the 1990s. At that time, most brokerage firms tended to have a "scarcity" mentality, which was really sad. In my firm, brokers rarely worked together; nor did they recognize the benefits of sharing clients or opportunities. And the only help I could count on was from an assistant I shared with three other brokers.

It was very frustrating. This should have been a total coup; after all, a total of $792 million in retiree money was paid out. I did manage to capture about $25 million of that from this opportunity, but it was only a fraction of what could have come to my business if I had been given the team and the resources to fully capitalize on the opportunity. The rest, obviously, went somewhere else.

What big lesson did I learn? If you are going to capitalize on big opportunities, you can't do it alone. You have to build a team.

BUILD YOUR TEAM

I have heard it said that there are two ways to create a business. One, you can be a technician, like Bill Gates, where you create a product and then hire salespeople to go out and sell that product. Or, second, you can be an entrepreneur like me, and surround yourself with technicians who work on the cases as they come in. In my case, those technicians normally did a far better job than me on the technical side of the business.

Clearly, either way to grow a business will work. However, as one of my mentors, Michael Gerber, points out in his book, *The E-Myth, Revisited,* a financial advisor must be three things when *launching* a business:

1. They must be the hunter/rainmaker/salesperson, the one who goes out and brings in the business.
2. They also have to be the manager. They must manage the financial planning process initially and eventually manage the people who work for them.

3. They must be the technician; they have to do the actual work of the business, which is creating the financial plan.

In the beginning, when you first start in this business, you have to do all of those things. Most of us tend to do all of those things until we reach our first "ceiling of complexity," a term coined by my coach, Dan Sullivan. This ceiling occurs when there are no more hours in the day and you can do no more to grow the business by yourself. This is the first great inflection point, where you realize that, in order to grow, you must hire other people to work for you.

If you excel at being the hunter/rainmaker/salesperson, then that's great; only a small percentage of people in the world actually have the hunter DNA. This skill is essential to building a business. If you can't continually bring in new clients, you won't be in business very long. Regardless of how satisfied you may be with the business you have now and your current income, natural attrition and commoditization of our industry makes it necessary to continually bring in new clients. As they say: "If a business is not growing, it is dying . . ."

Realize, however, that replicating your function as a hunter will be the most challenging part of growing your business. When you finally find someone who has that strength, it often and quickly becomes painfully clear that the new hunter's intent is to learn from you and then go build something for him- or herself. Because this is true, it is wise to have a rock-solid non-compete/non-solicitation agreement in place. Your first step should be to hire people to do the technical work of the business (to create the financial plans and to service the clients you bring in.) This gives you the bandwidth to bring in more and more clients for your team to advise and service. Once the team is in place and you have a stable of happy clients, you can put systems and processes in place so that your internal team can foster warm referrals from the existing clients they are helping.

The bottom line is this: If you want to grow your business, then you have to build a team. Hiring the first person is the most difficult of all the hiring decisions. It's also the one you should consider the most carefully. Your goal is to train one person and then have them train the second, third, and fourth employees. There are a couple of reasons why you want to build a team, but in the end, it's all about leverage. It's very difficult to "build the business of your dreams" with just you. Again, if it's all about you, then all you really have is a job; you don't have a business. If the business is totally reliant upon you showing up each day, then you don't have a business that has any intrinsic value. You just have a friendly boss . . . you.

To go into these concepts in much greater depth, I highly recommend that you read Michael Gerber's book, *The E-Myth, Revisited*. I agree with almost everything in that book. Several years ago, I was privileged to follow Michael Gerber as a speaker at an industry conference to outline the ways in which I incorporated his principles in my financial services business.

WORK *ON* YOUR BUSINESS, NOT *IN* YOUR BUSINESS

This is one of Michael's major themes: Building a team allows you to *work* ON *your business instead of* IN *your business.* This point is so important that I frequently reference these two quotes from Michael's book:

> "If you want to work in a business go to work for someone else, because while you're doing all the work you're not working on your business. You're not doing the strategic work of the business."[2]

and

> "Most people who own businesses in this country work far more than they should for the return they're getting. The problem is, they're doing the wrong work."[3]

The one thing I find interesting about the financial services industry is that you don't see many financial advisors who have what I would refer to as a bona fide business. Michael Gerber is the one who opened my eyes to this. So let me repeat: A business

---

2   Michael Gerber, *The E-Myth, Revisited* (New York: HarperCollins, 2001).

3   Gerber, *The E-Myth, Revisited.*

is not really a business if it relies upon you. If you have to be there every day, if you're the one meeting with all the clients, then you don't really own a business; you've simply bought yourself a job. If I were you, I would ask myself, "Do I really own a business or have I just bought myself a job?" Try not to fool yourself with that answer.

There's nothing inherently wrong with either answer to the question, but it's very difficult to grow a large practice and have the life of your dreams if your life is always consumed by doing the day-to-day work of the business.

LEVERAGE: THE MOST IMPORTANT CONCEPT

In his book, Michael Gerber wisely advocates comparing your business to McDonald's. He talks about the founder, Ray Croc, and the creation of the fast-food franchise model. Ray's company was in the business of serving fast food to large numbers of individuals. He started in one store and likely worked in that store, initially as the "hunter" (the one who brings in customers), the manager, and the technician. Ray Croc eventually grew the business exponentially by creating systems and processes to do the "work" of the business, and hiring people to run those systems and processes.

How does this apply to you? Well, if you want to build a business that can operate without your day-to-day involvement, you have to first build a team and then create systems and processes that allow your team to service your clients and run the day-to-day operations of your business. That creates "leverage," the most important concept to master if you want to build a large, successful practice.

To that end, I'd like to share some truisms my business coach, Dan Sullivan, shared with me that were eye-openers. I hope they'll be the same for you:

"If you want to make $300 an hour, stop doing $20 an hour work."

"You can do anything in the world as long as you're not the one doing it."

In our business, the clients need to be served. The question is: do they need to be served by you? I am living proof. I have a large practice with two offices, and there isn't one client who expects to work directly with me. In fact, through all the financial crises and calamities, I have received very few calls from clients. Normally, the only time I hear from a client is to give me a referral. But it wasn't always like that.

When I started in 1989 as a stockbroker, no one gave me any training on how to build a business. I was really a salesperson for my firm. The firm supplied my support staff, which was minimal. As I said earlier, I normally shared an assistant with three to five other brokers. When I asked for more help, it was generally denied.

In hindsight, I'm not sure why the firm didn't give me more support staff. They clearly cramped my ability to grow beyond myself, which couldn't have been good for the firm's revenue either. For the most part, the business was entirely dependent upon me. I did all the prospecting, met with all clients, entered all the trades, serviced all clients, even made my own appointments. The only thing the support staff did was home office paperwork. By 1997, I was making relatively good money but I was working twelve-hour days, seven days a week, and I was miserable.

That's when a friend of mine suggested that I join Dan Sullivan's program, Strategic Coach. I was in such a state then that I decided that I was either going to join Strategic Coach and figure out how to make this business work, or I was going to quit. The stress of doing it all was too much. I had hit my "ceiling of complexity." It didn't matter how much I worked or how smart I worked, I wasn't making any more money and I certainly wasn't taking any time off. In fact, in the first seven years I'd been in business I had never taken a day off, not even a Saturday or Sunday.

I joined Strategic Coach in 1998, and I participated religiously one day each quarter for the first three years, which is the "Master's" program. It was a wonderful experience, but at the end of the three years I can't say my business had exponentially changed. I was in the last day of my last class, my twelfth time there, and we did an exercise in which we stood up and picked a partner with whom to share our thoughts. I teamed up with a man named Paul. This encounter would forever change me and my business. We had started in Strategic Coach on the same day, and three years later, for all intents and purposes, I hadn't made any significant progress in terms of my business revenue. I think my revenue had gone from $300,000 per year to $400,000 per year.

Truthfully, I was happy with my progress because I had nothing else to compare it to. Until that day. Paul started reporting on his progress: When we first started in Coach, he was making about $300,000 a year. This year, three years later, he was on target to make $3 million! Additionally, he had transitioned from having a practice where it was all about him to being the owner of a financial planning business. His primary role was now that of rainmaker; he no longer met with clients after the first meeting. Instead, clients were served by his team. As a side note, his wife had just won a Body for Life contest, and he was planning to open a second business—a fitness gym!

I was floored. I thought to myself, "Where have I been? On what planet was Paul's Strategic Coach class?" Given the results he achieved, he was clearly on another planet than I was. Stunned, I said, "Paul, I am bowled over by what you've just told me. I don't understand logistically how you could have done all that. Could I come visit you and spend a day with you to pick your brain? I just need to understand the psychology of what you've done. I think if I can understand the psychology and how you've positioned these changes to your clients, then maybe I can do something similar." Graciously, he said, "Of course."

Within the next thirty days, I flew to Alexandria, Virginia, and spent the day with Paul. I found out so much that day that I was able to go back and implement many of his ideas. He was the one who suggested I read the book *The E-Myth, Revisited* by Michael Gerber. More importantly, he spent the better part of our time together talking about psychology and how he had successfully transitioned his clients from working with him to his team of very capable individuals.

A DIFFERENT WORLD FOR ME TODAY

Thanks to people like Paul, Dan Sullivan, and Michael Gerber, I play fewer roles in the firm today. Like Paul, my main function is to be a rainmaker. I continually try to create new and different ways to expose our firm to people who don't know about us. As we have grown, we have hired new "hunters" whom I train and mentor. As I said earlier, finding hunters who want to work within my firm has been a challenge, but it can be done. We have had to find people who want to build a "firm," not their own practice. Also, I continue to work with my management team to provide vision, leadership, and creativity. Annually, I work with the entire team to set goals for the business, including annual revenue and profitability goals. I am still the de facto leader of the firm but to the largest extent possible, I let my management team run the day-to-day operations. Clearly, when difficult decisions have to be made, the buck stops at my door, but I always ask my management team to weigh in on what they would do. My goal is always to "work myself out of a job."

Other than those limited activities, the business runs well without me, which is a testament to the great people I have managed to hire over the years. It didn't start out this way. It has been an evolutionary process. However, with patience and persistence, you, too, can build a business that can run day-to-day without your direct involvement. After all, isn't a business supposed to be the benefactor that allows you to live a great life? For most people, their business IS their life. I know; that's where I started. If that is where you are, here are some ideas on how to change that equation.

TEAM BUILDING

To create the business of your dreams, you must hire qualified people to work for you. Most on our team are Series 7, Series 65, and insurance licensed so they are legally allowed to discuss financial products with clients. Every employee—with the exception of our receptionist and our bookkeeper—must have the appropriate securities and insurance licenses to be part of my team.

In the beginning, there are a few things you will likely want to continue to do, at least while you build the infrastructure of your business.

1. **Bring in clients.** It is likely you will always be a primary rainmaker for your firm. Your job will be to find and sell your company's value proposition to good quality prospects. Be sure to clearly define your market and not waste time on people who don't fit the profile of your ideal client.

2. **Socialize with clients.** If you do things correctly, you will have positioned your business so clients enjoy working with qualified members of your team. Eventually, your licensed staff should be able to do nearly everything, including conducting quarterly reviews and making product recommendations. Although I have let go of these tasks, I have continued to socialize with our clients, something I very much enjoy doing. In fact, it keeps me connected to my purpose, which is taking care of people.

As I said before, it takes time to upgrade your business so that it works without your day-to-day involvement. It also takes a different mind-set: you have to be willing to let go of more and more and slowly relinquish the role of always being the "go to" person. (In the next chapter, I'll talk about how to make this transition more comfortable for your existing clients.)

When I first made this transition, I stayed very involved in the process in the first year. While I did not sit in on all client meetings, I generally did attend any meetings where new opportunities were likely to be discussed. Yes, I was reluctant to turn over the relationship to my licensed staff, but I had another purpose too. I felt like I needed to be in those meetings to critique the communication skills of my staff, which worked out well. After every meeting, we would discuss what went on in the meeting. I would point out obvious missteps and make suggestions for the next meeting. It took some time.

Also, one thing I have always enjoyed doing and still do today, is taking new clients out to dinner. Once they have implemented our plan, my husband and I will often take them to dinner. We enjoy breaking bread with our clients, and we feel it strengthens the relationship with our firm. It also gives me the chance to solicit feedback on our team and our process so we can continually improve.

As the "creative genius" of the business, I still participate in the strategic planning of the business. I'm always looking for the next "big thing" for the business. The next big thing may be a new financial product that has been created in the marketplace; other times it may be doing joint venture marketing with other professionals. I also love spending time training and motivating my team. It's so gratifying to see my team members grow in their knowledge and skill.

MY TEAM MEMBERS ARE MY PARTNERS

When it comes to our team, I try to treat all team members as if they were my business partners, because in essence, they are. Here is my advice to create that environment:

1. Always back your team even if it means letting go of a client. Your team is more important than any single client.

2. Let your team members do their job. Don't micromanage them. Your team will rise to the level of your expectations and, with a little encouragement, will greatly exceed your expectations.

3. Give up some control. I think the main reason people don't progress is because they cannot give up control.

4. Create a way for your team members to participate in the profitability of the business. My team members are rewarded based on the success of the firm. All team members have a base salary, but after one year with the firm, they participate quarterly in the profitability of the firm.

5. Help team members understand their primary function is to give you the tools necessary to make it easier for your new prospects and clients to say "YES."

Hire people who have opposite skill sets to your's. We use the Kolbe Index (www.Kolbe.com), which has proven very accurate and useful for our group. We always want our staff working in their areas of strength; we do not want them trying to work on their weaknesses.

1. Make sure that team members understand their ultimate job is to free you, so you can focus on four things:

   ◦ Find new relationships.

   ◦ Socialize/break bread with existing relationships.

   ◦ Get the prospects or clients to say yes.

   ◦ Take a lot of time off.

2. Be sure you have a well-drafted non-compete/non-solicitation agreement that all employees sign. I spent a lot of money on this, and it has saved my bacon on more than one occasion.

I'm a firm believer in the Dan Sullivan mantra that, *"Time off is a prerequisite, not a reward."* In the last two years, I've skied more than thirty days, taken the entire summer off, and not been at the office unless there is a reason. I can do that because I have a team motivated by the bottom line. Because of the way we compensate our people, I never have to worry about productivity. If the firm is not making money, it will ultimately impact each member of the team. It's not like when the "cat's away, the mice will play," because if the mice play, their compensation at the end of the quarter will be less than stellar.

The bottom line is that I position myself as the founder and CEO of the business. Clients understand they are buying the services of the firm, not me. They must agree to work with various members of our team. We continually market the strengths of the entire group, and more importantly, we market our process and our philosophy of money, Lifestyle Driven Investing™.

From the day they come on board, each client is introduced to their relationship manager as well as to the other members of the team who have been identified as being integral to the success of their process. All members of their team begin to interact with them from day one. In particular, it is the relationship manager's job to shepherd the client through the process. We have very specific steps in the process, and it is the relationship manager's job to ensure the standards of our process and our firm are upheld.

In the end, we try to put ourselves in our clients' shoes. If the client thinks they are buying me, what happens to the client and their financial situation if something should happen to me? If I get hit by a Mack truck, does the client have to find a new advisor? I don't ever want the clients to rely solely upon me or any one person in our firm, not from day one and not ten years down the line.

WHERE TO START?

So, where do you begin? Find one person. Require they get all their licenses and then have them sit in on every meeting and on every phone call. Teach them how to do your asset allocations, your plans, whatever your business requires. They should screen all your calls, and when they are trained, they should be able to take care of all servicing issues and eventually even give advice. (Again, they need to be fully licensed to give advice.)

Then, as your business grows, if they want to be given more responsibility, they have to find and train their replacement. THAT IS THE KEY. Give them the task of creating the job description;

posting the job; doing the interviews; and once the new person is hired, doing all the training. Each subsequent employee has the same responsibility if they want to move up in the organization.

When should you hire? As soon as you are able. I don't believe you can grow or be successful on your own. I was lucky that my husband believed in me; even before we could really afford to hire someone, we did. We took a chance. It turned out to be the best investment we have ever made. Hiring a full-fledged team has increased the value of my business more than any other investment we have ever made.

TRANSITIONING YOUR CLIENTS TO YOUR TEAM

So, how do you help clients who are used to working with you become comfortable working with a member of your team? They are accustomed to having you pick up the phone, meet with them, and go through their quarterly or annual portfolio reviews with them. How do you get them trained so that they are not only "okay" working with your staff but also delighted to be doing so?

The first step is to direct all servicing calls to a member of your team. The easiest thing to do from day one is to never answer your telephone. That's how we started. My assistant would answer the phone, and the client would say, "May I speak to Erin?" She would say, "Erin is in a meeting, or Erin is unavailable; may I help you?" The client would express their concern or ask their question. My assistant would say, "Well, I will go ask Erin and get right back to you with her answer. I'll try and catch her between meetings."

Sure enough my assistant would come to me, tell me what the query was, and I would recommend they do (x) instead of (y). Then my assistant would call them back and relay the message. Eventually, my assistant just answered the questions. She knew what I would say or recommend. If she was unsure, she would certainly check with me beforehand. She was fully licensed to give the answer, and the clients were normally satisfied with her answer. Occasionally, at the beginning, clients STILL wanted to hear from me, but that was rare and never happens today.

The next step I took was never taking a meeting or conference call by myself. I always had a staff person with me on the call or in the meeting. If it was a conference call, I would say something like, "Suzie is going to be here taking notes, and she'll get back to you with the proper forms to execute the trades (or whatever)." In the course of the call or meeting, I very intentionally kept deferring to the staff person who was with me in the meeting.

If I happened to answer the phone by accident, and the client had some type of service request, I would put them on hold and then come back and tell them I had no idea how to handle their issue. That was the job of another team member. This is when I very intentionally got "dumb" in the business. I would imply I had no idea how to get that check cut from their account or send them that IRA distribution form. I always told them that I would ask my assistant, Joe, to take care of it immediately. In the future, instead of calling me to get an IRA distribution form, they would naturally call Joe.

When it comes to service items, like forms or check requests, you should never know the answer to, nor be able to assist with, the service issue. You should only know the answers to questions about the bigger items like investments, strategies, or other big-picture matters. Always defer to the staff person, even if you know how to send out a distribution form. At first, you may have to "pretend" you don't know how to do it; otherwise, you may continue to be asked to do things and you will never get out of working IN your business.

If you want to build the business of your dreams, then you have to hire, teach, and rely upon others to do practically everything. You might as well start with the little things, the servicing items.

RULES OF ENGAGEMENT

The next thing we did was type up our "rules of engagement" so there was never any question as to how we work. We actually call this piece the "Expectations of Our Engagement," but internally we called it the ROE. This is a three-page document that acknowledges we understand they have relationships with other advisors. They have other stockbrokers, bankers, and CPAs, and each of those other advisors has a unique way of doing business with them. Some of them pick up their phone right away, some have voicemail, some have secretaries, and some return calls within twenty-four hours or the next day.

In this document, we clearly outline how we do business. For instance, in the rules it states that by engaging our services, they agree to work with various members of our team. They agree that they will be serviced primarily by a relationship manager, who will guide them through the process. It's clearly laid out in our expectations of engagement document that I will know what is going on with their case at all times. I don't want them to think I have completely abdicated my role in the firm. I just don't have to be in all the meetings in order for the client to be well served.

The document also states the three ways we get paid:

1. We get paid a fee for doing the plan. That fee is based on the complexity of their case and is a one-time fee, paid up front.

2. We expect to be paid on implementing the plan through product fees, referral fees, commissions, or assets under management fees.

3. We rely on the active goodwill of our clients. If they're happy with the service and experience they've had with our group, then we expect that they will agree to introduce us to their friends and associates who may need financial planning.

We are very clear in the expectations of engagement that we rely upon our current clients to introduce us to our next clients. We tell them we do no national advertising and our entire business grows through personal referrals from satisfied clients.

We also discuss our expectation that they will become renewing clients with our firm. We are not looking for one-time customers but clients who will stay with our firm for decades to come. We tell them we will always strive to exceed their expectations and ask for permission to check in with them every twelve to eighteen months for honest feedback as to how we are doing. We set up the expectations for a future meeting ahead of time, telling them we will ask them to give us a grade on a scale of 1 to 10 on how we are doing. If it's anything other than a 10, we want constructive feedback as to what we could do to get that score to a 10. We are also clear with every engagement that we do not do any "transactional business." A prospect cannot come to us and say, "What would you do with $1 million?" Unless they hire and pay us to create a financial plan, we will take a pass. While we prefer to engage clients by doing a comprehensive financial plan, including a review of their estate planning documents, etc., we also have a second tier of engagement called an "Investment Only" plan. From a liability standpoint, I would *urge all* advisors to have a policy wherein you protect yourself from making investment recommendations without really knowing your prospect's entire financial situation. Since litigation is so rampant, I can't emphasize this strongly enough.

Finally, make sure to set out the expectations of engagement in advance. This is the best way to ensure that clients clearly understand the relationship so there are no misunderstandings.

QUESTIONS TO PONDER:

- **Have you reached the limit of where you can grow your business on your own?**

  There are limits to what one person can do in growing a business. If you've reached that limit, and even if you haven't, it's probably time to hire other people to work for you. You cannot grow a business that runs without your day-to-day involvement if you have to be involved in every aspect of the client engagement.

- **How can you build the best possible team?**

  Hire people to do the technical work first. Your goal is to train one person and then have them train the second, third, and fourth employees. Be sure you have a well-drafted non-compete /non-solicitation agreement that all employees sign.

- **Are you ready to transition from salesperson to business owner?**

  Once you've built the team, it's time to leverage your team members by creating an environment where the client is served without you being involved in every step of the process. After a period of transition, the best thing you can do is intentionally hand off your credibility to your team members. Highlighting your team member's credentials and overtly telling clients how valuable that team member is to your firm goes a long way in easing a client's mind about working with someone other than you.

- **Have you developed your own "rules of engagement" for your business?**

It's certainly worth your time and energy to set up expectations about how you have set up your business, including a section outlining your role in the business versus the roles of your team members with whom the clients will work. We are very up front in our initial meeting that all clients must agree to work with various members of our team. The ROE also lays out how we will get paid, our expectations for client referrals, how customers can deliver feedback, and so on. It sets the stage for your relationship with the new clients and prevents misunderstandings later on.

For more information and additional resources, go to www.sevenfigurefirm.com

CHAPTER 5

USING SYSTEMS AND PROCESSES TO CREATE RAVING FANS

The right systems and processes—and vigilance about maintaining them—are *essential* if you want to grow a large practice that doesn't depend on you. The more things are systematized, the less chance things will fall through the cracks and the greater the likelihood that clients will have a consistently superior experience with your firm.

SUPERIOR AND CONSISTENT CUSTOMER EXPERIENCE

We create every system and process in our firm with the client experience in mind. Consumers are heavily influenced by the experiences they have as they make a purchase. Nordstrom knows this. Nordstrom customers know that if they need to return something today or next year, they will have a similar experience, a transaction with no questions asked. Interestingly enough, consumers and clients are also creatures of habit. If they liked the experience, they want to have that experience repeated over and over and over again. Changes to the experience, whether good or bad, can alter the way a client perceives your business.

By way of analogy, consider the habitual nature of people who go to church. They tend to sit in the same section of the church each week, in the same pew, and usually around the same people, because they want consistency of experience. One of the reasons McDonald's is so successful is that people can go to a McDonald's anywhere in the world—whether, say Alamogordo, New Mexico; New York City; or Munich, Germany—and have a very predictable experience. The cheeseburger will be warm or hot, and it will taste virtually the same as the last one they had, no matter where it was consumed.

The same principles apply to our business. It is important to create systems and processes to (1) define the experience you want your clients to have and (2) assure that experience is repeated over and over again. You don't want your clients calling or coming in each time and having a different experience; it really changes the nature of their relationship with you.

How do you do this in practical terms? Here are some examples. Make sure every team member answers the phone the same way. Set up the conference room in exactly the same manner every time. Greet customers in the same way, regardless of which staff member is giving the greeting. If you know your clients' drink preferences ahead of time, serve them their drink of choice without them having to ask.

Clients are likely to sit in the same seat in your conference room each time they enter. We like to control where the clients

sit the first time they come in because we know they will gravitate to that same seat the next time they come. Therefore, we
have a system that determines where we want them to be seated
the first time they enter our office so that we can optimize their
experience with us.

If there is a husband and wife, we always seat the woman at the
head of the table and her husband on the side that does not face
the door of the conference room. Why? One, because we want her
to feel like she has some control in the meeting and to see herself as
someone who has something vital to contribute to the discussion.
Two, we do not want the male client distracted by anything going
on in the hallway outside the conference room. Since we have glass
windows, we try to keep the distractions to a minimum.

Often the woman will not readily accept the seat at the head
of the table, so I explain to her it's much easier on me to have her
there and her husband directly across from me so I don't have to
end up with "tennis head," turning my head from side to side
if they are on opposite sides of the table. That usually works.
Another tactic is to make sure the receptionist serves her drink
at the head of the table so she knows that spot was prepared for
her. The extent to which you create consistent experiences will be
the extent to which your clients feel comfortable coming in and
referring others to you.

SYSTEMS CONSTANTLY EVOLVE

By now, we probably have hundreds of systems and processes,
but it's taken decades to come up with all of them. Obviously
as we changed brokers/dealers and moved, hired new positions,

etc. over the years, we have had to refresh our systems. It's like cleaning the rooms of your house. By the time you clean the last room in your house, the first one you went through needs to be re-cleaned. I'll go through a couple of systems we have established so you can see the ones we consider the most important.

A SAMPLING OF OUR SYSTEMS
Client Meeting Agendas

We create a written agenda for every meeting, beginning with the first official meeting we have with the client. More than anything, the agenda is for our benefit so we (1) remember everything we need to discuss with the client and (2) have backup evidence for the file that covers what we discussed in the meeting. The client's version of the agenda only shows broad categories and provides space for taking notes. The advisor's version of the agenda has detailed notes from prior calls, meetings, and/ or discussions to remind the advisor of important details he or she may not recall. For instance, the advisor's copy will likely have the names and ages of all family members. There will even be notes on personal information the client has shared, such as whether there is a new baby in the family, an impending retirement or vacation, the death of a dog, whatever is important to the client. It strikes an amazing chord with the client, when you make mention of something that is vitally important to them. Of course, there is no way any of our advisors can recall all those details for all their clients. The only way you can do this effectively is to create a system to serve as your memory.

In the first couple of meetings, the agenda might be three pages long, because we have a lot to cover. We will discuss the client's risk management profile, their current estate planning documents, their balance sheet, and spend time reviewing investments and insurance, etc. We want to be sure the advisor is set up for success and doesn't come out of the meeting without covering all the important items with the client. The agenda keeps the meeting very focused. Anything that wasn't covered in the current meeting will be moved to the next agenda.

Client Seating System

As mentioned earlier, consistency of experience is of utmost importance to us. Therefore, our conference rooms are always set up with water and a writing tablet with a pen at each seat. And, to repeat what I said earlier, if it's a husband and wife, then we seat the wife at the head of the table and have the husband seated on the side of the table where he will face the least amount of potential distractions.

Two-Minute Warning System

We have our "two-minute warning" system for arriving clients. We have a bell that rings in the back of the office when the front door opens. We instituted this before we had an official receptionist sitting up front, and it serves us now if the receptionist is away from his or her desk. (Our receptionist is often my assistant or the assistant to other advisors, so he or she is often seated out of sight of the front door.) Once that bell rings, we expect someone to greet our guests within two minutes or less and lead them into one of our conference rooms. We don't want clients sitting in our waiting room without having been greeted. (Ideally, we don't want them sitting in our reception area chairs at all.) It is office policy that every person on the team has to be listening for that door. If the receptionist is on the phone or in the restroom, it is up to another team member to get to the front door within two minutes to greet our guest.

Whoever greets the guests escorts them to the appropriate conference room and will also take their drink order. If they are already our clients, we keep track of their drink preference. As the receptionist seats them, she will typically say something like, "Would you like a Diet Coke?" or, "I see you take black coffee," or "Do you still take your coffee with cream and two sugars?" Clients love it when you remember them and their drink preference. We want the environment in our office to be more like Cheers, where everybody knows your name. It is also our policy that the clients are never left alone in the conference room. A staff member will stay there and chat with the client until the relationship manager arrives.

The Ritz-Carlton Experience

As a part of our training, we have sent several members of our team to the Ritz-Carlton Experience training. The information, systems, and techniques they bring back to share with the group are invaluable. We have adopted many of the tools used by The Ritz-Carlton. For instance, we have a Monday morning meeting each week, similar to The Ritz-Carlton "lineup," where one member of our team shares an inspirational quote or delivers a positive message. We recognize "atta girls" or "atta boys" among the team for great performances the previous week.

We have a Botsford credo and a list of twelve service values that we live by. We try to instill the idea that we are "ladies and gentlemen serving ladies and gentlemen," just as they train employees to do at The Ritz-Carlton. Most importantly, everything we do is filtered through a corporate lens that asks the question, "How would The Ritz-Carlton do this?" For instance, when we serve our clients lunch, it is on nice china with cloth napkins? We serve water or soft drinks in nice glasses versus in cans, plastic bottles, or paper cups. We even have a signature scent in the office so it is familiar each time clients enter. As time goes on, we adapt and evolve our process. Where we used to just have traditional pens and paper in the conference room, we now have pens with a stylus on the end in case our clients want to take notes on their iPad or iPhone.

Who Will Do What by When?

At the end of a meeting, we always want the clients to know who will do what by when. We never want the clients to leave the meeting without knowing what the next steps are. We want them to know that we will contact them next and when that will be, or that the ball is in their court and we expect a call back from them. Generally, we won't leave the ball in their court. We like to control the contact, so most often we'll schedule the next meeting or call right then, while we have them in front of us. If the clients leave the office and it is not clear who will do what by when, the relationship manager will send an e-mail outlining the next steps.

Download System

Another system we rely on—to make sure we type up a good and accurate synopsis of every call and every meeting—is the "Download System." Each relationship manager is responsible for providing a very thorough download of everything that happened in the meeting or on the call. Sometimes our relationship managers like to type their downloads; some like to use a transcription service such as Words Express. Some of the relationship managers take copious notes on their iPad in iNotes. Regardless, the office policy is that within twenty-four hours, all meetings and calls that have taken place will be downloaded into our customer relationship management (CRM) system and become a part of the client's permanent record.

We have adopted a uniform format for our downloads. The first part of the download lists who was in the meeting. The next section contains all the tasks to be completed. Some of those tasks are immediately assigned to others on the team to be completed. The relationship manager completes some follow-ups, but all are outlined in the download. The third part of the download provides a clear description of what took place in the meeting and any decisions that were made (i.e., similar to the minutes taken at any meeting). If there were investment products discussed, the download also includes any disclosures that were made regarding things like liquidity features, risks, fees and charges for the product, etc. The relationship manager can also use his or her download to help create the next meeting agenda. It is a body of notes that captures the essence of every call or meeting.

Daily Phone Logs

Another system that we use is our "daily phone logs." The daily phone log is a record of every call and/or servicing issue that takes place and any e-mail that comes in or goes out. All of this is posted to the client record. Many years ago, the staff would simply create a Word document and pass it around. At the end of the day, they would either e-mail or fax it to me wherever I was, so I could see what happened during the day. Technology has certainly allowed us to evolve. Now, all the downloads end up in the client's permanent CRM record, and at exactly 5:01 p.m. a report is generated that outlines all e-mails and all calls that came in or out of the office. Everyone on the team has access to these phone logs in case they want to know what happened on a given day.

Answering the Phone—Greeting the Client

We try not to use voicemail. We try to catch the phone by the second ring. I hate voicemail and think it's very impersonal, so we want our clients or prospects to be able to talk to an individual. We have a policy that we return all phone calls on the same day. We also have a policy wherein a client is always referred to as Mr. and/or Mrs. until they have specifically asked to be called by their first names. Even if they give permission for one person on the team to call them by their first name that does not imply any other team members have the authority to refer to them by their first name. Each member of the team has to be personally invited to call a client by his or her first name.

Covering for Team Members

We require everybody to have access to everyone else's business e-mail. Hence, we ask our team members not to use their Botsford Group e-mail for personal business. This allows for ease in backing up team members when they are in meetings or out of the office. As often as possible, whoever serves as the backup checks the colleague's e-mails. If they see an e-mail come in from a client, then we like to immediately respond to the client and say something like, "Mr. Smith, I see that you've sent Joe an e-mail. Joe is in a meeting right now but I'll be sure he gets your message or e-mail and responds to you in a timely manner." Clients want to be acknowledged. They don't necessarily need to have their issue resolved or question answered immediately, but they want to make sure their e-mail was received or their phone message was acknowledged. To the greatest extent possible, we're pretty fast on the draw, and we try to get back to them as quickly as possible.

Birthday Acknowledgment System

We think it is very important to acknowledge our clients' birthdays. It is the one day each year that we can honor them with a phone call and a birthday card. We have a process for each.

Birthday cards

Each month, one of our employees downloads from our CRM system a list of which clients have birthdays that month. She handwrites the envelope and places a real stamp on the envelope. About three to five days before our client's birthday, the card is mailed.

Birthday calls

One of the first e-mails generated each day by one of our employees is a list of all birthdays for that day AND for the next day. It is our policy that all clients are called on their birthdays by their assigned relationship manager before 10:00 a.m.

A newer system we have recently begun using is the "Birthday Lunch." We get a list of all the birthdays for the month, and the relationship manager chooses which of his or her clients to take to lunch. We usually pick clients we enjoy spending time with and those we would like to replicate. It's always fun to work with the friends and associates of our best clients.

Recently we have begun focusing on clients who are not as close to us on a personal level, and it has completely changed the nature of our relationship with those clients. It's amazing what a meal honoring a client's birthday can do! To make this happen, one of the assistants makes a call to schedule the lunch. As a present, we order a *Time* or *Life* magazine that was published in the week of their birth. The magazines can be purchased at www.papermags.com. The clients have LOVED getting a real magazine in its original condition that was published in the year of their birth. We have received a lot of great feedback on that, in addition to a lot of goodwill and referrals. As of this writing, our referrals are up almost double since we started these birthday lunches with the magazines.

Client Brochure Assembly Process

We have a written system for things like the client brochure assembly process. This system outlines what marketing materials go into our marketing packets, down to the order of the piece and whether they are placed on the right side or left side of the folder.

Tiffany Wine Referral Glass Process

Each new client who contracts with us is sent a classic Tiffany wine glass they can use to drink wine or their morning juice. This is a small token of our appreciation for their business. In a letter we send with the glass, we let them know that we have also sent the same type of glass to the person who referred them to us. Sometimes we send Tiffany wine glasses to several people: anyone who mentioned us to them or had any influence in their decision to hire us. We also outline our Tiffany wine glass program in this initial letter and hope that, during the course of our relationship, they will collect many wine glasses by referring many people to us.

I know this seems ridiculous, but the Tiffany wine glass program has been a huge success. I once had a client who seemed to call every Monday to give me the names of new prospects I should call that week. My response was always, "Dennis, you must have had a party this weekend and broken a few glasses!" It always made for a good laugh. Once a client has received twelve classic red wine glasses, we move to white wine, champagne, and even tea glasses. Fortunately, we have had clients who have sent us so many clients over the decades that we have been able to stock their china cabinets with beautiful glasses.

New Client Onboarding Checklist

From the time a client engages with us, we employ a checklist and a process for our initial engagement with them. For instance, the minute the contracting paperwork comes in, an e-mail goes to the client acknowledging receipt of their check and introducing them to their new team. In addition, clients are given a copy of the Steps of our Process so they know where they are in the planning process. As soon as that e-mail goes out, the assigned team follows up with the new client to be sure they have their contact information. Each step of the process is well defined for maximum efficiency.

Referral Thank You Process

Any time we hear that our clients are talking about us, we want to acknowledge their effort on our behalf. We handwrite thank-you notes for all referrals, regardless of whether the referral becomes a client. In addition, our clients will receive a small gift in the mail (usually it's some form of candy or cookie, but it could be golf balls or whatever that particular client is interested in).

CREATING SYSTEMS IS TIME WELL SPENT

These are just a few of the systems and processes we use. It is important to note that I always knew having written systems and processes would be significant; I just couldn't find the time to sit still long enough to map them out and write them down. Eventually (and unfortunately) I was forced to do so in the early 2000s.

At the time, we were a very small team; less than five of us. My personal assistant's husband was diagnosed and eventually died of brain cancer. Through no fault of her own, my assistant was out of the office on a very frequent basis to go with her husband to doctor's appointments and attend to his needs in his final days on this earth. Finally, she stayed home with him full time for the last four months of his life, which left us with a gaping hole in our office.

My assistant knew how to do everything. She was a wizard when it came to making things happen. Unfortunately, all that information was in her head, which didn't do me any good when she was out. As she sat with her husband as he slept, I asked her to start typing up everything she did from the time she walked in the door until the end of the day. I continued to pay her even though she was out so she was very willing to help us in any way she could. I told her I needed her to write down everything she did in such detail that a monkey could do it.

Eventually, I hired a male temp and one by one, I asked him if he could follow the systems she had listed. For instance, for the birthday card process, I made her get into her own head and type out: "This is how I figure out which clients are having birthdays. I go to the CRM program, I enter the field I am looking for, I print out this field, and I type up a list. Then I go to 'X' website and order the birthday cards. When they come in, I do 'Y.' This is where I order stamps; this is where I keep the stamps. This is how I address the cards. There is a box on my desk with the days of the months on it. After I address the envelopes, I put the cards in the slot of the date that is five days ahead of the client's birthday. Each morning I pull out the cards to be mailed, etc."

It was an arduous process, to say the least, but we got twenty or thirty systems created during that awful time in her life. She said it was a godsend having something to think about, and it was certainly a godsend for us.

Now we just have to improve on the systems we already have in place and create new systems for new things we want to do. I hope you are able to create your own systems and processes before you have to. Let me assure you, being proactive is a better way to go.

QUESTIONS TO PONDER:

- **Have you created systems and processes at your business so that everything is streamlined and consistent for every client?**

  Consider applying systems to meetings, client seating, greeting clients, customer service, assigning responsibility for post-meeting tasks, case notes, phones, e-mail, client onboarding, and client birthdays.

- **Which systems and processes should you document?**

  If you are having trouble getting started on this, just start asking questions. Questions like: "How, specifically, do we greet clients? How do we seat clients in the conference room? How do we send birthday cards? What is our system for sending out IRA distributions? Every question that comes up indicates there is a process that should or could be documented.

- **When did you last review your current systems to see which ones could be scrapped or needed to be refreshed?**

  If something's not working well for your clients, then it may be time to rework your existing systems so that nothing falls through the cracks.

  For more information and additional resources, go to www.sevenfigurefirm.com

CHAPTER 6

PSYCHOLOGY AND PERSONAL DISCIPLINE

I f I could change one thing about the training program I went through at my first broker/dealer, I'd make sure there were classes on the psychology of sales. In fact, there were many times I wish I'd gotten my degree in psychology instead of business, because so much of what we do involves psychology.

Consider this: The quintessential task of a financial advisor is to identify a path for the client to follow. We create a plan. It usually involves purchasing investment or insurance products. Sometimes it involves working with other advisors like CPAs or attorneys. We all know the plan isn't worth the paper it is written on if the client doesn't take action. We also know clients don't always take action or agree with our plan. Why? We think we created a perfectly good plan that will lead to the exact outcome the client has articulated. Why doesn't the client just go along with it? That is the $64,000 question.

In my career, I have more than once literally scratched my head and asked myself, "What happened? How did I get this so wrong?" I have learned over time that there are a number of key concepts to understand:

1. Prospects often have preconceived ideas of who you are and what you do. In order to differentiate yourself from your competitors, you have to quickly change any preconceived notions; otherwise you look just like the last advisor with whom they met.

2. Clients may not be able to articulate what they truly want from you.

3. Clients don't necessarily want your best answer immediately; they tend to appreciate it when you walk them through the process so they can arrive at the same conclusion you have.

4. Women approach financial services with different expectations and needs than men do. Therefore, you have to approach women differently.

5. If you want to win over both members of a couple, you have to show how a plan meets both of their needs.

6. Don't ignore or patronize the female partner in a couple.

7. If you are a female advisor who works with male clients, be careful not to intimidate the man's partner.

8. Don't use language that's too advanced for your prospects or clients.

THE PRECONCEIVED NOTIONS
OF PROSPECTS

The first thing I always teach advisors when I am coaching them is this: When a new prospective client walks in the door, he or she likely has a preconceived notion about who you are and what you do, largely based on the last person they met who called themselves a "Financial Advisor." For some prospects, their only experience has been with a stockbroker, so they think you'll be just like the last stockbroker they met. Some have only dealt with life insurance agents, so they assume that you're going to be just like the last life insurance agent they met. Unfortunately, this is likely true for everyone in our industry. People often have preconceived notions, not only about who we are but how we think and what we'll likely recommend for them. The first thing you have to change, as quickly as possible, is that perception.

Also keep in mind, most people maintain the perception that someone who holds a juris doctorate (an attorney) is extremely smart and therefore held in the highest regard. After the attorney, someone who holds the title of CPA (certified public accountant), is often considered the second most credible advisor. I always joke that the next person in the credibility pecking order is probably the Mercedes dealer, followed by us, their financial advisor.

As I mentioned in my introduction, some of this perception arises from the actual barriers to entry in each of those professions. The attorney, whom clients or prospects hold in highest regard, has gone through college and law school and has passed the bar exam. The CPA has gone through college, perhaps gotten a master's degree and sat for the CPA exam. The Mercedes dealer? We don't know how much schooling he's had. The financial advisor, other than taking the Series 7 test and maybe the Series 63 or 65, hasn't had to clear the same hurdles as the attorney or the CPA, so it stands to reason why prospects might regard us as "less than" their other professional advisors. The first thing we have to do is prove to prospective clients in a short period of time why we deserve to be given the same credence as their most trusted advisor(s).

CLIENT PSYCHOLOGY 101: UNDERSTANDING WHAT YOUR PROSPECTIVE CLIENT TRULY WANTS

What does your prospective client REALLY want? That can be a very tough question. Sometimes what they tell you they want is not what they really want. Sometimes they don't know what they really want. Other times, what they want isn't available in the real world. Have you ever had someone tell you they were VERY risk averse, but they also wanted to beat the S&P 500? I've had people say they wanted to beat the S&P 500 but to make sure their principal was guaranteed and completely liquid.

In my firm, I work mostly with retirees, people who are age fifty-five and older, who have worked for thirty-five to forty years. I have had to learn to read between the lines and interpret what they really want. I have learned that, for the most part, my clients want to be able to do what they want, when they want, with whom they want, and not worry about their money. The degree to which I can help them not worry about their money is the degree to which they will either hire me (if they are a prospect) or keep me (if they are a client.)

On the other hand, your target market might be accumulators who are willing to take a little more risk. They want accelerated rates of return. They have an entirely different mind-set, so if you start talking to the accumulators about something as boring as bonds that don't represent accelerated growth, you'll lose them.

I'm firmly convinced that if you want to be successful in our business you really have to understand the mind-set of the person sitting in front of you. At the end of the day, your job is to get the client to say "yes" to your recommendations. Presumably your recommendations are the precise prescription to get the clients to the place they told you they wanted to go. To get there, they need to take action. It is your job to help move them along that path. As such, they NEED you to read between the lines of what they are saying and what they are not saying. They NEED you to figure out what makes them tick. They NEED you to figure out what they are afraid of, because they are likely not going to tell you. The extent to which you can understand their psyche is the extent to which they will say "yes" and you will become their trusted advisor.

A COUNTERINTUITIVE WAY TO GAIN CLIENTS' TRUST

I had been in business for over twenty years, yet I missed something that eventually came back to haunt me. From about 1995 until 2008, I was fortunate to work with a group of executives from one Fortune 500 company who were all connected to one another and also very good referrers. The phone would ring and the new prospect would say, "My friend Joe says I should work with you." The strength of those warm referrals cannot be over-stated. With a strong referral, generally the new client believes your advice to them will be similar to the advice you gave to their friend. Often, when you get a warm referral, there is very little pushback when it comes to product implementation.

Unfortunately, these clients were in Atlanta and I lived in Dallas. After thirteen years of commuting between the two cit-ies, I made a decision in 2008 to stop traveling as much and to build a network of new clients in the Dallas area. These were all brand new prospects, and I did not have the benefit of trust that comes with a warm referral. But I didn't realize that at first. I used the identical process for these new clients and expected to get the same results. Because my advice was sound and ide-ally suited to these new clients, I was befuddled as to why they gave me so much pushback when it came to implementing the investment products.

I knew something was wrong, but I couldn't put my finger on it. I finally decided to ask one of these new clients, a woman who had also become a good friend to me. My client (I'll call her Susan) had been in both the commercial and residential real estate business for her entire thirty-year career. She had gone through our financial planning process, and when I asked her why she and other new clients hesitated to implement my firm's recommenda-tions, she was able to immediately articulate the reason. What she said was eye-opening.

She gave me this analogy: "Erin, when I was new to the commer-cial real estate business, people would call up from all parts of the country and describe to me over the phone the type of commercial real estate space they needed. They would say they needed fifty thousand square feet, wanted a downtown location with this amenity or that. By the time I got off the phone, I knew exactly the right space for them. After all, I was a professional and I knew every property that existed in the Dallas area. The representatives from the company would fly in, and I would take them to the space I had in mind. Every time, they were astounded at the degree to which this space matched exactly what they had told me over the phone. They were excited and, by all indications, they were interested in leasing the space I showed them. But then they'd get on the plane and with very few exceptions, they would get 'buyer's remorse' or start wavering in their decision to lease the space."

Susan said it took her awhile to figure out what was going on. She could commiserate with me because I was experiencing the same thing. I knew exactly the right investment recommendations to make for each new client, just as I had known the exact formula for all the warm referrals who had come over the years. But these new people, who didn't come from a warm source, were hesitant to take my advice. In fact, I lost three in a row. Why?

Susan then proceeded to tell me what she learned and how it applied to what I was experiencing. She said, "Erin, let's use the example of residential real estate. When I was in that market, my greatest desire was to find my buyers the perfect house for themselves as quickly as possible. If I could spare making them look at twenty houses and only have to look at two, I thought I was doing them a favor. So I would work very hard and try to select the perfect houses for them; I could drive them directly to what I felt were the one or two that were best suited for them. Each and every time, the buyers agreed I had nailed it. My expectation would be that they would sign a purchase agreement, and we'd be in escrow within a few days. But each and every time, the buyers would get buyer's remorse. Why? Because although buyers trusted me, they wanted to ensure *themselves* they had seen every single home that remotely met their specifications.

"In their minds, they would say, 'I know Susan showed us two properties that were amazing and completely met our requirements, but could there be other homes that were even more right or more amazing for us?'"

The same held true for Susan with her commercial real estate clients. The company representatives felt responsible as agents for their firms to make sure they had seen ALL office buildings that could have met the company's needs, not just the ones Susan showed them. Here's how Susan relayed her experience as a client with us. She said, "Erin, when my husband and I engaged your firm, I'm sure you knew by the time we left your office the first time we met the exact investments you were going to recommend for us. You are a seasoned professional, and you know what our situation required. But here's the problem: We didn't know. Just like the people who want to drive around and see every house that meets their real estate requirements, we wanted to 'drive around' and see all the potential investment products that could meet our requirements. In a sense, you went right to the first house—the perfect house for us—but you didn't give us the chance to drive around and see all the other houses so we could see for ourselves how perfect your recommendations were."

I was never so grateful to anyone. As a result, I created an entire process based on the idea of driving my clients around to see every investment so they could be a part of the process of narrowing down the final recommendations. We call this part of our process our "Investment Collaboration" process. We have an entire meeting dedicated to going through all the various types of investments that are out there—in broad general categories—and giving our clients the chance to learn, provide feedback, and be a part of the overall *collaborative* process. We have found this collaborative method gives the clients a sense of ownership in the final outcome presented in the plan. In the end, we normally arrive at the same place we would have gotten without this meeting, but this process gives our clients the confidence that comes from knowing they have reviewed the alternatives themselves and come to the same conclusion as their advisor.

THE PSYCHOLOGY OF WORKING WITH WOMEN

If you are working with a married couple, the biggest mistake you can make as a financial advisor is to discount, marginalize, ignore, or talk down to the wife. It is a HUGE mistake, but one I see over and over again. I have coached many financial advisors on this issue and have come to the conclusion that most people in the industry are clueless as to how to deal with female clients. You might think this is only a problem when the client is a single woman. That couldn't be further from the truth. The bigger issue is how women who are part of a couple are treated. To me, this shows a complete lack of understanding as to who the actual decision maker likely is in the relationship.

What you should never forget is that it is the woman, in almost every case, who makes all the decisions! That comes as a surprise, doesn't it? Okay, I'll soften my stance just a bit: *It is the woman who retains ABSOLUTE VETO power.*

I'll give you a personal example. Many years ago, my husband, Bob, and I built a house and decided to put a pool in the backyard. Bob called me one day and said the gentleman who was building our pool wanted to meet with both of us to talk about the number and type of pumps that would be required for our pool. I immediately said, "No honey, you can handle that; I'm not really interested in dealing with that subject. Whatever you decide is fine with me." But my husband said, "No, this man really insists you be there for the meeting; he wants to talk to both of us." Reluctantly, I agreed and made a point of leaving my office at 3:30 p.m. so I could attend the meeting.

At precisely 4:00 p.m., the gentleman arrived and spent ninety minutes talking to us about pool pumps. The problem was, he never once looked at me or acknowledged I was even in the room. It was so unbelievably rude. I was furious! Believe it or not, I didn't say anything. I sat there and thought, "This is such a great lesson." The meeting ended. We showed him to the door. I shook his hand and was very kind, but as soon as he left, I looked at my husband and said, "Nope, that's not going to happen. We are not buying anything from that man." My husband looked at me incredulously and said, "Are you kidding? The man just spent an hour and a half with us; he has a great product." I said I didn't care if he had spent half his life with us. He was condescending; he ignored me entirely, especially after insisting I attend the meeting. There was no way I was going to reward that behavior by giving him his next sale and that was the end of it. VETO!

From my perspective, there's absolutely no question about who runs the show, or at the very least, who has absolute veto power in a couple. The degree to which you acknowledge that reality is the degree to which you'll be successful in winning with couples. This shouldn't come as a shock. Our society recognizes the power women hold, something that is even acknowledged in a few adages, such as, "If mama ain't happy, ain't nobody happy." Funny as it may be, I remember what my husband told my son when he got married: "Son, the only two words you need to learn to have a successful marriage are, 'Yes, dear.'"

Here are some other pointers that might be helpful to know regarding the woman in a couple. As much as a woman says she doesn't want to be at the meeting, sometimes she really does want to be there. Either way, you have to make the woman feel like she is a valued part of the process. You have to engage her on the heart level, not just the numbers level. I tell the wife I very much appreciate her coming to the meeting, and as I have said before, I seat her at the head of the table. I tell her that her input is incredibly valuable; something that is, in fact, underscored by my seating her at the head of the table. If we are doing estate planning, I tell her I will not conduct that particular meeting unless she is present. I really go out of my way to make her want to be there and be an active participant. I also tell both of them I don't expect them to learn everything I know. I tell them they will probably only remember ten percent of what we talk about, but what I do want is for *both of them* to leave with a sense of confidence that we know what we are doing, that we will listen intently to what each of them have to say, and that we will do our best to respect their time. I stress to her, in particular, how grateful I am that she cares about their outcome and, as a result, I will do my best to deliver the best possible solutions.

Because I'm a woman advisor who works with couples, I also face another challenge: Sometimes women prospects can be a little intimidated by another woman. I don't know why that is, but I have observed this on enough occasions to know it merits mention. In my experience, this mostly happens with women who have chosen to stay home and raise their families. I highly respect that as the most difficult of all careers, but the woman may not know me or know I feel that way. If you are a female advisor and you sense this "tension," there is a simple thing you can do to help the woman in the couple feel completely at ease with you.

Make it a point to focus on the woman at the beginning of the meeting. Give her almost all your attention, while giving her husband just a glance now and then. Keep focusing on her until you sense the barrier has melted. That is what I do. I go out of my way and overtly give the woman nearly one hundred percent of my attention until I have her nodding her head in agreement with me. When I know she and I are on the same page and that she not only doesn't feel threatened by me but also has come to believe I have her best interests at heart, then I will bring her husband into the conversation. Until that time, my attention is on her.

I suggest male advisors take the same approach. Seat the woman at the head of the table and engage her from the very beginning.

Even if she shrinks back and lets her husband do most or all of the talking, stay aware of her presence at the table and keep her engaged in all parts of the discussion. Treat her in a way that lets her know that you understand she is ultimately in charge of the meeting's outcome, because in all likelihood she is. I can assure you that before the garage door opens on their return trip home, she will have her say about whether or not you will be the couple's next advisor.

The other thing I do—when I sense that the wife (or in some cases, the husband) doesn't have much knowledge of financial planning—is to speak at the level of the lowest understanding in the room. In any meeting where we will be discussing industry concepts, I will always preface my comments by telling those present I'm going to be speaking at a fifth-grade level. I tell them I am not doing this to be insulting or patronizing; I just want to be sure everyone in the room is on the same page and is tracking with me. As soon as I can see they're with me, then I will raise the level of how I speak to them. As such, I'm never condescending, but I also don't want to talk over anyone's head. Talking over someone's head does nothing to impress them. You just lose them and the opportunity to get the outcome that is best for your client. Be aware, of course, that it is not always the woman in the couple who has less financial knowledge. I have worked with many high-powered female executives whose husbands were the less-knowledgeable parties.

WHAT WOMEN WANT

If you want to get a better handle on what women want from financial planning, consider these surprising findings from a recent study done by Allianz. This European financial firm found that forty-nine percent of women—"across all corners of life and affluence"—fear ending up broke and homeless. What is truly stunning is that this "irrational fear" (Allianz's term; not mine) is found among the twenty-seven percent of women with annual household incomes above $200,000![4]

According to the survey, the statement, "Deep down, I have a fear of becoming a bag lady," holds true for fifty-six percent of single women, forty-three percent of married women, fifty-four percent of divorced women, and forty-seven percent of widowed women.[5] It's also true for nearly half (forty-six percent) of women Allianz considers "financially savvy and financially empowered,"[6] even though these women are "generally less worried about their retirement savings."[7]

Given the findings, you can assume a typical woman never wants to be placed in a situation where she feels that something could go wrong with her finances or that the rug could be pulled out from under her.

Women are generally not huge risk takers. If they are going to take risks, they want the risk/reward profile to be well articulated.

---

4   "INSIGHT 5: 'Bag Lady' Fears Persist Among Even the Most Successful Women," Allianz Life's Women, Money, and Power Series, accessed July 22, 2016, https://www.allianzlife.com/retirement-and-planning-tools/women-money-and-power/bag-lady.

5   "INSIGHT 5."

6   "INSIGHT 2: The Rise of 'Women of Influence.'" Allianz Life's Women, Money, and Power Series, accessed July 22, 2016, https://www.allianzlife.com/retirement-and-planning-tools/women-money-and-power/women-of-influence.

7   "INSIGHT 5."

They definitely want to know the downside of any plan presented to them. I've noticed that very few women are comfortable rolling the dice when it comes to their investments. That said, women tend to make very good investors. They do their homework, and their expectations tend to be very realistic. They're not looking for home runs.

Single women, especially, tend to make very good investment decisions. Because they are alone, they don't have a safety net. They know it's up to them, so they usually do their research. Once they set their minds on a strategy, they tend not to second-guess it.

I wish I could say the same about widows. As a female financial advisor, I have found that it can be challenging working with widows. The widows we encounter in my firm are usually over sixty-five years old. Most have played a traditional role in their marriage. Typically, the husband was the primary income provider and the one who took care of their investment decisions.

A widow who comes from these circumstances will often bring in one of her sons, who then acts as the decision maker. If not, she goes back to her husband's financial advisor, typically a man. I can understand this. She has always had a man managing her money and finances, so it probably gives her comfort to continue this pattern. If you look at this dynamic from a psychological standpoint, male advisors have an edge with this clientele. If I were a male advisor, I would certainly consider older widows as a potential target market.

I have had male advisors ask me if I think it is a mistake for them to go after the female market. I say, "Absolutely not." I think male advisors have a great advantage when it comes to women clients. There is already a belief that the financial world is dominated by men (which is true), so it is not so far-fetched that many women would assume a male advisor would likely have more of an aptitude for finance. The biggest thing any advisor who works with women has to remember is to never talk down to a woman or worse, ignore her. Make sure her concerns are addressed and she is made to feel like an integral part of your process. If she has a spouse or partner, treat her and her partner as equals.

A NURTURING NATURE

Finally, let me admit I take advantage of the fact that I *am* a female advisor. As a female, it is assumed I have a nurturing nature. That very much appeals to women prospects and clients. With all clients, I spend an entire appointment letting them talk about themselves. Who doesn't like to talk about themselves? I ask probing questions. I want to know all about their family of origin, where they were raised, what they were taught about money. I want to know all about their parents, siblings, nieces, and nephews.

We call this meeting our Visions and Values Conversation™. It is an opportunity for prospects and clients to talk about what's important to them. I tell them I am looking for one of two things: potential "train wrecks," or opportunities in lifetime or at death to take care of the people or causes that are important to them. This is the kind of touchy-feely conversation that I imagine is more comfortable for female advisors than male advisors.

In these conversations, I have had male clients break down in tears as they talk about disappointments in life or failed expectations or any number of missed opportunities. They feel comfortable opening up because I have provided a safe space for them to openly share their deepest emotions. I have not heard many stories about men doing this in front of other men; it just isn't done. I'm not sure that matters in the overall scheme of things, but it is quite a privilege to have a grown, successful man feel comfortable enough to be that vulnerable in your presence. It creates a bond that is not easily broken.

THE PSYCHOLOGY OF WORKING WITH MEN

I don't know how it is for other female advisors, but generally speaking, I find male clients easier to work with than female clients. I'm not sure why this is, but I don't think it's that much different than in other areas of life. It seems to me that men, typically, are just not as complicated as women. I always joke that most men are happy as long as they have a big screen TV and a remote control. My husband would add a cold beer to that equation, but that's about it! But that's not to say they don't have their own needs and expectations for the financial planning process.

While women tend to want financial security, men tend to be bigger risk takers. They want to talk about the home runs; the big hit; the next big deal; or the double-, triple-, or ten-bagger. Just like they like to drive fast cars, men want their investments to be fast and furious. Why is that? In my opinion, the DNA of men and women is vastly different. (I use that term casually, not scientifically.)

From the dawn of civilization, men (in most hunter-gatherer societies, at least) have been assigned the role of hunter. Their job was to bring home the bacon. Her role was to fry it up in the pan. In many parts of the world today, this is still how things work. Regardless of how much has changed over the centuries, I still believe these differences are hardwired in men and women, to some degree. A man expects to go to work, be the provider. He has done it all his life and knows if the chips were down, he could do it again. That's why he isn't predisposed to worrying about running out of money. His internal DNA says if he runs out of money, he'll go make some more.

This is just not so for women. As I mentioned earlier, it has been well documented that women fear running out of money more than just about anything else. Hence, there's an art to working with couples. You have to address both of their deep-seated needs. If you only appeal to the woman and her need for safe, safe, safe, then you will bore the man to death. If you start talking about the next start-up opportunity or the new hot deal, then you may get interest from the man, but you will often lose the woman.

To overcome the inherent clash of needs, you have to acknowledge the differences in their inherent natures. You need to point blank tell the woman your plan is going to take care of her. She needs to know that all her security needs will be met. At the same time, you need to assure the man you will also meet his need to have some Vegas money or to drive in the fast lane. The sooner in the conversation you can bring these points to the forefront, the better; otherwise, you're going to lose one or the other of them.

As I said before, men do have fears. However, you will generally not get that from him in a meeting with his wife. Normally, the only time you'll get a sense of what the man fears is when he's by himself and you put him in a safe environment. What I have found from the many, many conversations I have had with male clients over the years is that even the most successful men fear disappointing the people around them, the people that depend on them. A lot of times men feel that they've been put on a pedestal and they're supposed to have made all the right decisions, all the right moves, and they're supposed to be the caretakers of their families.

The last financial crisis has been very hard on men. They did their best to do well by their families, only to lose a lot of money in real estate and the stock market. So many men base their entire identity on their position as the leader of their family or the status of their job. When they lose a lot of money or feel they have made terrible mistakes (or worse yet, get fired), they fear the potential loss of status more than anything in the world. Overall, men don't require a lot to make them happy, but losing the respect of their families or status among their peers is a huge issue for most men. They will go to great lengths to protect themselves from that type of loss.

If you're a male advisor working with men, it's easy. You have such a clear advantage because men do business on the golf course and in other social settings. I've seen my male colleagues leave the office on Wednesday afternoons—the afternoon doctors traditionally take off—to pick up a golf game with a bunch of doctors. In general, I think you men are much better at networking with each other and setting up introductions. Men have no problem calling another man and asking for an introduction. I belong to a couple of professional women's groups in Dallas, and we have often discussed this clear difference in the way men and women network. We decided there was significant value in having the "good old boy" network.

ADVICE FOR WOMEN ADVISORS

As a female advisor who was practically a "pioneer" in the financial service industry, I know only too well the advantages and disadvantages of being a woman in this business. In the course of my career, I generally refused to give in to any stereotypes about my place as a woman in the industry. I have never allowed myself to see or acknowledge a "glass ceiling;" in my mind the only ceiling that existed was in my own head. Because I was an entrepreneur who never received a W-2 paycheck from an employer, my ability to make the same as any of my male counterparts was certainly within my own control. The commission schedules were the same; the payouts were the same, etc., so I never felt I couldn't compete on equal footing with men, or make myself an even stronger competitor if I chose. That being said, there were some prospecting methods I felt were not well suited to me.

Let's take golf, for instance, which we know works so well for men, I admit I thought about taking up golf as a way to meet potential clients but ultimately ruled it out. As a woman, I did not think it would be wise to show up at the golf course on an afternoon in the hopes of picking up a golf game as a fourth with a group of men. Why? First, having a woman join the game would likely change the nature of the men's experience on the course. Rather than being able to spit and cuss on the course, (along with other things my husband said are probably not appropriate to mention in this book), most men would naturally clean up their act to accommodate a woman playing with them. They might not like that; after all, it's their afternoon to play and be "themselves."

Second, if I did go golfing with three other men, I have to imagine their wives wouldn't be too excited to meet with me after that. I can just envision the conversation at home: "Honey, I met this amazing woman golfing today. She was out there by herself and happened to join the three of us men for a round of golf. Oh, by the way, she is a financial advisor, and I really think we should meet with her." I can only imagine the wife's response.

At one point, I did consider taking golf lessons and playing in the weekly women's nine-hole golf outing. Then I realized if I were going to do this, it would have to be solely for the love of the game, not because I wanted to use it as a prospecting tool to meet female clients. Why? Because there is an unspoken rule that would have likely worked against me. Care to guess what it is?

Let me give you a hint: What is the one question that's never asked of a woman by either a man or another woman?

Stumped? Most people would be. I have noticed, however, that no one ever asks a woman, "What do you do?" It's taboo. That's because no one wants to put a woman in the position of possibly having to answer, "I don't do anything." Or "I'm a homemaker."

I have a funny sideline story to prove my point here. My husband and I have gone to five of his high school class reunions—the tenth, fifteenth, twentieth, thirtieth, and recently his fortieth. When we left the last reunion, I told my husband I couldn't believe that, in all the reunions we attended, not one person I spoke to at any of the functions has ever asked me what I did for a living. They all knew my husband was an airline pilot, but not one of them knew about my work. They didn't ask! I'm a woman—I swear asking the question is still taboo!

In short, if you are a female financial advisor golfing with men or women, the topic of what you do for a living would likely never come up in conversation. You could force the topic in both situations, but I doubt it would be comfortable in either setting, and it just might be off-putting. That's why I suggest you only take up golf if you truly love the sport, and not because you think it would help you market yourself.

If you are a female advisor who works with or prospects to men, here's another "sand trap" that requires careful thought and a careful approach. If the man is a part of a couple and you want to do business with the couple, go out of your way to make sure the woman in the picture never feels threatened by you. I remember when I was a younger advisor in my early thirties. I wanted to cut my hair short and spikey and wear interesting, fashionable clothes, including short skirts, to the office. A mentor of mine said, "You know, Erin, it's your prerogative to wear what you want outside the office. However, inside the office there's too much at risk if you become a threat to anyone, especially to a man's wife or an office coworker."

I realized he was right. That was great advice. From that day forward, I went out of my way to dress very professionally and one might add, a little on the "frumpy" side. As a result, I have never been a threat to a prospective female client. I could also count on the fact that my male prospects were looking at my eyes and listening to what I had to say; rather than distracted by cleavage or a short skirt. You certainly don't want the wife walking out thinking, "So, she wants my money and my husband!" That would not be conducive to your business relationship with any couple, so do not do—or wear anything—that could lead the woman to think this way.

OTHER PSYCHOLOGICAL FACTORS TO KEEP IN MIND

When dealing with prospects or clients, the maxim, KISS (**K**eep **I**t **S**imple, **S**tupid) always makes sense. I spoke at length, earlier, about why it is so important to make sure you are using language that can be easily understood, no matter how little knowledge your prospects or clients have of financial planning. You never want to be condescending, but you also don't want to talk above anyone's head. That's not the way to impress people. In fact, you lose their attention and the opportunity to get the best outcome for your client.

Also be careful to not baffle clients or prospects with industry jargon. If you don't know the answer to a question, don't make it up. It's much better to say, "That's a great question and frankly, it's been a long time since anybody's asked me that. I'll refresh my memory (or find out the answer) and get back to you." Clients appreciate the fact that you don't know everything. Anybody who tries to come off as if they know everything is usually exposed quite quickly.

Again, there are times when it is to your advantage to play "dumb." As I said in an earlier chapter, I actually try to under-whelm clients with my own knowledge because I want them to lean on the members of my team, not me. Very often, I will end the first meeting with a prospect by saying, "Now you know everything I know! From this point forward we'll bring in experts in all the areas that are relevant to your situation." I make it clear that the smartest thing I have ever done was to hire people smarter than me.

Clients are better served when they are not coming to you for everything. More to the point, that is the only way to build a business that can work without you. In the end, your responsibility as the founder and owner of the company is to make sure everything that is promised is done and done by people who have expertise in that particular area.

THE KEY TO IT ALL—TELL YOUR STORY

Clients will only do business with you and take your advice if they trust you and believe you have their best interests in mind at all times. As investment guru Nick Murray has often said, "Clients don't care what you know until they know that you care." I can't tell you how strongly I agree with those words. You really do have to care about the outcome for your clients. If you can't demonstrate that you care about their outcome, they aren't going to listen to anything you have to say.

One way to establish trust is to tell your own story. I try to tell my story as early in the relationship as I can, for good reason. I realize in the course of our process, I am going to ask them a lot of very personal questions. I have to, in order to do a good job. If I am to protect them and find out what they care about, I have to know nitty-gritty details about them, which many times includes the hidden dirty laundry known as family problems. Everyone has things they'd prefer to keep hidden; it's just a matter of how long it takes to uncover them.

The risk of not uncovering these hidden issues early in the relationship is that they will often come back and derail even the most meticulous plans you could have created to help your clients reach their financial goals. For instance, it would have been nice to know their son was in drug rehab; you could have set aside funds to handle future stays in rehab or other complications. It would have been nice to know that your client's mom was likely going to have to move in with them, which would require their current house to be retrofitted to accommodate her wheelchair. All those dirty laundry items have potential negative consequences for your clients' lifestyle.

I always tell clients, "I don't like surprises. I want to make sure we have considered every single thing that could come along and derail your plans." That is easier to articulate, once you have opened up and told your own personal story and perhaps revealed a couple of crazy aspects about your life.

In the beginning, that wasn't so easy for me to do. If you read my personal story in an earlier chapter, you know that my early years were full of tragedy and misfortune. Once I got through that period, I did my best to forget all that had happened. As such, I never told my story to anyone—not my friends, associates, and certainly not to prospective clients. I was ashamed of my personal background and didn't want people to know where I came from or how I got to this point. What a big mistake!

What caused me to tell my story was an actual prospect couple who came in and started describing what had recently happened in their family. Their son had been involved in a car accident with a motorcyclist in which someone was killed. I could see the toll this was taking on them. They felt guilt and fear. They were worried about losing their assets in a potential lawsuit, since the son had been driving their car. As I heard their story, I began to shake. It opened up an old wound and took me back in time, causing me to relive all those emotions. It felt like someone had just ripped a Band-Aid off an open sore. But, I knew what I had to do. I had to tell them the same thing had happened to me. I had to share with them that while their son felt like he would never laugh again, he would. Time would heal those wounds.

I found myself going through the drama and the details of my story, but more importantly, I noticed an immediate change in their demeanor. I wasn't just some uninterested third-party consultant. I was sharing in their humanity. I was relating to them on a very deep and personal level. What I realized that day was that prospects and clients want to work with REAL people, not glitzy salespeople. They want to relate to an authentic, caring individual. Their money is *personal* to them, just as their hopes, dreams, and fears are. The sooner you can relate to them on a real and personal basis, the sooner they let down their guard. It is then that trust begins to take hold.

Here's another example: A couple of years ago, I was asked to meet with another financial advisor whom I did not know. I wasn't sure why we were meeting, but a client wanted me to meet her so I agreed. When we walked into the restaurant, I could immediately sense that this woman was very intimidated by me. Her body language said it all; her hands were folded firmly across her chest, and she wouldn't look me in the eye. In our awkward first minutes, I found out she was a divorcée and a financial advisor who presumably specialized in working with other divorced women. That being said, it was like pulling teeth to get that information out of her.

When I tried to ask her some basic questions about her area of expertise, she gave me one-word answers. I still hadn't figured out why I was there, but I began to suspect that her friend may have thought I could be a good referral source for her or perhaps a mentor of sorts. Since she was so closed off to me, I figured that she was probably very closed off to her prospects and clients as well. I decided to try a little experiment and said, "Okay Kate, tell me about you, like how long were you married?" I was thinking since her expertise was supposedly in divorce matters, she must have been married—perhaps a good place to start. She responded by saying, "I don't think that's relevant or important."

Her answers to all my simple questions were borderline combative. It was clear I wasn't making any headway with her. Asking her questions wasn't going to help me develop this relationship; that was certain! I finally said, "Okay, maybe it would help you if I told you a little about me and my background." As I began telling my personal story, I could see her demeanor and body language change immediately. All her defenses came down and her arms opened up. A conversation began. Because I knew she was new to the business, I took the liberty of offering her some unsolicited advice. I said, "Kate, let me tell you what I just experienced in our meeting. When I arrived at this restaurant, you were clearly closed off to me, based on your obvious body language. You gave me one-word answers to everything I asked. Some of your responses were borderline combative. That was, until I decided to take the first step in trying to form a relationship with you by opening up and telling you all the gory details of my life.

"Here's what I observed: Once I opened up to you, you felt comfortable. I let my guard down, so now you feel comfortable." She started nodding in agreement. I said, "Let me tell you something about growing a financial services business. You said you're trying to grow your practice, and you want to work with divorced women. Don't you think they've experienced some of the same things you have and don't you think the very first thing you're going to need to do is tell your story so they know you can relate to them? I can tell you right now, if you behave in the manner you just behaved with me, your career is never going to work. Your prospects will likely be just as closed down as you were with me. How are you going to help them if you can't get them to talk? You are going to have to be the first to take off all your proverbial clothes and expose yourself to your clients. I call this 'getting naked first.'"

Kate had an overwhelming reaction to my comments; she started crying. The idea of opening up and exposing herself to me, or in particular to her future prospects, had never occurred to her. She said the idea was actually frightening. The story of her divorce was so painful to her, yet she quickly saw that allowing herself to be vulnerable would give her the greatest opportunity to actually relate to and eventually help her prospects. Since then, she has told me dozens of times how helpful that little piece of advice was for her. She admitted that she couldn't understand why female prospects were not opening up to her. She hadn't connected the dots. That was a huge breakthrough for my friend Kate.

EVERYONE HAS FEARS

Here is another example of the power of a personal story. A few years ago, I was given the opportunity to speak in Austin to a group of people whose minimum net worth was $50 million. They were members of a local group who met on a regular basis to hear new ideas. This day, I happened to be their speaker. From the moment I walked in, I sensed a really negative vibe. The body language of the attendees was so obviously closed off, I had to ask myself why they were even there. It was clear most of these people had been to dozens or hundreds of free lunches and dinners. Their body language told me they assumed they had heard every idea on the planet and they felt my speech was going to be another worthless presentation, as so many of the previous presentations had been. It was almost as if they were being polite just by attending. Mind you, I don't get opportunities to speak to one hundred people, all worth more than $50 million, all that often, so I was pretty intimidated. Fortunately, I had my silver bullet with me. I had my story.

After a brief but awkward start, I began telling my story. I talked about the fatal car accident I was in at age sixteen and my fear of being sued or worse, ending up in jail. I talked about my mother's fear of losing our only asset, our family home. I knew each of these people in the audience had a large net worth, they probably had children or grandchildren who drove cars or boats in their names, and they probably hadn't done adequate asset protection planning. Fortunately, asset protection strategies were my topic for this speech. What is always interesting in our business is that regardless of the net worth of the person sitting in front of you, on the other end of that $50 million balance sheet is a real person.

Once again, I watched the atmosphere in the room shift. Soon, audience members were engaged in my topic. It was as if they suddenly realized that essentially we were all the same. Maybe they'd gotten lucky and their business had been successful, but they all had the same general fears. After the presentation, I had so many great conversations and wonderful feedback. I found out some of the people in that audience feared they might accidentally invest their money with the next Bernie Madoff. Some worried that leaving all their money to their children would ruin them. Some were worried to the point they had bodyguards to protect their children from being kidnapped.

Interestingly enough, they all had worries and fears in common; it was the type of things they worried about that were different. The bottom line: everyone has fears. The degree to which you can connect with other people's humanity, including their unspoken fears, is the degree to which you have the basis for having truly authentic conversations and, ultimately, relationships. This is how to use psychology to create the optimal outcome for the client.

You need to be ready to tell a lot of stories. They need to be real stories; but keep in mind, *they don't have to be your own story*. Not everyone has a rags-to-riches story like mine. It doesn't matter. The stories just need to be relevant and to the point, not random or self-serving. The clients must be able to relate to those stories. Otherwise, it can be disastrous; so don't pull stories out of your back pocket that are totally irrelevant to the discussion just for the sake of telling a story. My best advice is to pay attention along your journey so that you're picking up relevant stories that you can share with the next person down the line.

PERSONAL DISCIPLINE REQUIRED

It should probably go without saying that a tremendous amount of personal discipline and dogged determination are required to achieve a high level of success in our business. I'm sure that could be said about any industry. As I said earlier in this book, I realize not everyone wants to be at the top of the heap. For those who do want to make it to high levels in our business, the concept of personal discipline cannot be ignored. In fact, I believe it must be mastered.

I had to create routines and rituals for me to stay focused because things like follow-through are not in my DNA and therefore not my strong suit. That being said, I was fortunate to have an internal combustion engine that thrived on achievement for achievement's sake, so it didn't take much to motivate me.

One thing I learned early was that I had to be very judicious with my time. When I started, I had a five-year-old at home and a husband who was commuting in and out of Panama City, Florida, from Dallas. Essentially, I was a single mom for the first couple of years in the business. I will go into the disciplines I established later on, but suffice it to say I was up early in the morning, took my son to his private school, and then began my day of prospecting. I knew every minute counted, so I tried to arrange meetings like my Out-to-Lunch Bunch for breakfast, lunch, cocktails, and/or dinners.

In the early years, cocktails and dinners were virtually out because I had to pick my son up from day care, but all other times in the day I had to be very focused. I was totally serious about building my business. The one thing I did pretty religiously was to leave my office by 4:30 each afternoon so I could pick my son up at the after-school day care center. More than anything in the world, I did NOT want my son to be the last child picked up. I can honestly say he never was.

Once I got home, I was "mom" until 8:00 p.m. when he went to bed. From 8:00 on, I went back to work (from home), doing paperwork and following up on things from that day or the previous days. I would fall into bed around midnight and get up and do the same thing over again day after day, week after week. It took that kind of commitment to make it. I still think it takes that kind of commitment. I still work very hard and put in long hours.

SUNDAY NIGHT DISCIPLINE

If there was one discipline that I think made ALL the difference in the world, it was my Sunday night routine. To give you some background on how this ritual came to be, it is helpful to note that from the time my son was in junior high until he left for college, I cooked the same meal every Sunday night. He and his good friend, Whitney, convinced me to cook roast beef, mashed potatoes, gravy, and corn for anywhere between twelve and twenty-five people EVERY Sunday night.

The people who came were neighbors and friends. They knew to let me know by Saturday night if they would join us so I could take out one, two, or more roasts from the freezer. On Sunday morning before church, I would peel the potatoes and have them in a pot on the stove. After church, I took about a one-hour nap. The rule was—everyone came at 6:00 p.m. and left by 8:00 p.m. *with the dishes done.* Otherwise I couldn't have pulled it off week after week. They also knew that five minutes after they left, our son went upstairs for the evening and I went back to work.

I didn't leave my home, but I got out my briefcase and started planning for my next week. I would go through all my e-mails from the week before to be sure all of them had been answered. I would consolidate notes from my yellow legal pads and make sure I had downloaded all my meetings. I would gather up my receipts for lunches or dinners from the previous week and get them ready, with their appropriate IRS explanation, to give to my bookkeeper (who was my husband for a lot of years). I then got out a brand new legal pad and started planning my week. I always had my top twenty prospects listed and my top twenty centers of influence to contact. The first page of my legal pad listed what I was going to do the following week; the pages subsequent to that were my questions or assignments for the team. My goal was to be completely finished and organized for the week by 11:00 p.m. I would then go outside and have a glass of wine and read something non-business related, like a cooking magazine, to take my mind off the work that lay ahead.

On Monday mornings, the alarm rang at 5:30 a.m. I have never worked out on Monday mornings; although, I have frequently attended evening yoga or other exercise classes. I often left my home at 6:30, depending upon traffic, because I wanted to be the first one at the office and ready to rock and roll for the week.

For years, I went to a Marriott Hotel next to my office, where I reviewed my notes and got ready for the week.

At precisely 8:00 a.m., our team would meet for an hour or so to go through the items listed on my pages and pages of notes. By the end of that meeting, the team knew what they were supposed to work on and what outcomes I expected to see. For me, the sense of confidence I gained by being one hundred percent organized every Monday morning was worth every minute I spent on Sunday night. I couldn't have achieved what I have without that routine.

Years later, after my son left for college, I did not do the Sunday night dinners anymore. Instead, I began my workweek around 6:00 p.m. so I could finish closer to 10:00 p.m. Also, we have transformed the Monday morning meetings substantially; now all team members are responsible for being prepared for the week. I no longer come in and tell them what they should do. In fact, we now start the meeting thirty minutes later (at 8:30), and a different team member leads the meeting each Monday.

By 8:15 a.m., each team member is responsible for going into our hard drive to fill out what we call our "At a Glance." Each team member writes what they did the previous week, and they write what they will be working on in the coming week. The business has evolved enough that I don't have to tell them what to do. We have professionals who know the steps of our process and know what they need to get done. Nevertheless, it gives me confidence to see this sheet in writing by 8:30 a.m. every Monday morning. I know every member of the team knows what they are supposed to do that week, and it gives me a chance to ask questions or redirect their time if I know of a more pressing issue.

YOUR ULTIMATE OUTCOME
IS UP TO YOU!

Within the first year, I learned many lessons, most of which were painful. One of the hardest things for me to wrap my arms around was that I was pretty much on my own to sink or swim. Thank God for my friend, Hal, because he was not only my mentor but also my only real friend in the office. The other brokers initially liked me when I was new and nonthreatening. They were as convinced as my manager that I was going to fail. After all, I was twenty-nine, female, blonde, and new in town. I swear the office staff took bets on my demise and went out of their way to help me reach that conclusion.

I was never quite sure why people were so hell-bent on seeing me fail. It took many years before I figured it out. The truth is that most people are satisfied with mediocrity and anyone who rises above mediocrity is seen as a threat. Most people are not willing to do what it takes to achieve tremendous, outrageous success. It is hard, and it takes too much effort. Most people choose the path of least resistance and bristle at anyone who chooses to go down the road less traveled. For whatever reason, I have always chosen the road less traveled. What I have found is that all the "goodies" are at the end of that path. However, choosing to do what others will not do can be rather lonely. There are not always a lot of cheerleaders along the way. During the years I have counseled other producers, I have often made these two observations:

1. It is lonely at the top.
2. If it were easy, everyone would do it.

I don't know where you are in your career path. You may be satisfied with where you are and if so, congratulations! Keep doing whatever you are doing. On the other hand, you may wonder what it might be like to reach a higher level of productivity and financial success. You might be curious to find out what "goodies" are waiting at the other end of the rainbow. I'm not sure what drives you. For me, it has been two things:

1. Being able to help our clients create or maintain their preferred lifestyles and, equally as important, helping them protect their legacy for their loved ones. Knowing how hard our clients have worked for their money and how much they love their families inspires me to do the very best I can and be the very best person I can become.

2. Having a lot of money to be able to help my family and contribute to the charitable causes I am passionate about. Being able to influence the outcomes and the lives of others who have not had the advantages I have been afforded is a huge motivator.

That's it. That's what I live for and what drives me every day.

How about you? What drives you? I raised this question in chapter 1, and I am returning to it here because it's *that important.* You have to figure out what you're going to do with the money and what impact you want to have; that's what keeps you focused. Without that, you'll peter out in a hurry. The winds of discouragement will blow you over unless you are *passionately committed to something bigger than yourself.*

If you have a big enough WHY to sustain you, then it's easier to keep your momentum. So figure out what will drive you when the going gets tough. If you are very clear about that, then the rest is easy.

QUESTIONS TO PONDER:

- **Do you really understand the mind-set of the client sitting in front of you?**

At the end of the day, your job is to get the client to say "yes" to your recommendations. Presumably your recommendations are the precise prescription to get the clients to the place they told you they wanted to go. To get there, they need to take action. It is your job to help move them along that path. Consider making the journey a collaboration between the clients and you.

- **Are you telling your story, or other people's stories, so that your clients can relate to you?**

To connect with other people's humanity, you may need to show your vulnerable side first. Telling your story (as long as it's relevant and not self-serving) is one way to do that.

- **What are your weekly rituals that will keep you disciplined?**

You cannot grow a large practice or reach higher goals unless you are personally disciplined. I will restate: my Sunday night ritual was probably the single greatest step in making sure I hit the ground running on Monday morning. Setting up your personal rituals and disciplines cannot be overstated.

- **Are you passionately committed to something larger than yourself?**

Figure out what drives you so that you can stay disciplined and focused.

For more information and additional resources, go to www.sevenfigurefirm.com

CONCLUSION

I am Kay Lynn Mayhue, a woman who has had the privilege of growing up in the financial services business under Erin's mentorship. I ultimately became her business partner and am now the president of Botsford Financial Group.

I hope you have enjoyed the book.

I can assure you what we have done WORKS, and it can be DUPLICATED. If you want to take your financial services business to the next level and break through any barriers you are facing, open your mind to the ideas presented in the previous pages.

With that said, I thought it would be helpful to provide a summary of the elements I have found absolutely critical to success in our business. I speak from the perspective of someone who, early on, made it her mission to study success. I have observed hundreds of advisors, looking for the answer to questions such as: What are people in the top ten percent doing that those in the rest of the industry are not?

Based on what I've learned, I'd have to say that the secret recipe for success in our industry—when pared down to its most essential ingredients—would read like this:

RECIPE FOR SUCCESS

Start with a huge focus on
marketing and **prospecting**

Wisk in **unique tools** that define your **brand**

Add the use of **leverage**—hiring the
right people doing the right things

Constantly stir in consistent service and
experiences through **systems and processes**

Blend in a ton of **personal discipline**,
persistence, and dogged determination

And TA-DA—you have a success!

Let's look at each, one more time, to help you remember them.

Marketing

This is a word that can mean many things to many people. My definition of marketing is simple—getting butts in seats! You might have the most amazing brochure explaining your services, but it is meaningless if no one reads it. You might have a terrific website or have the most amazing investment strategy on the planet, but if no one knows about it, it is worthless.

You have now read about some of the strategies that have worked for us to get those butts in seats. Ultimately, you need to figure out what you are willing to do to make this happen. Is it cold-calling, giving seminars, doing a radio show? Is it direct mail flyers, asking for referrals, print advertising, or joint marketing with other professionals? Whatever marketing method you decide on, the key to success is sticking with it for at least eighteen months. Every one of those marketing methods works IF you can keep doing it over and over and over with unwavering discipline and dogged determination. So before you run out and update your website for the twentieth time, or spend two hours a day reading *The Wall Street Journal*, ask yourself if you should really be spending that time and money getting the butts in the seats first. You don't need to know what's happening in the markets if you have no one with whom to share that information!

Branding

Once you have those butts in seats, you only have a short period of time to differentiate yourself from every other advisor the prospective client has met. As Erin has said previously, every prospect comes to you with a preconceived notion of what you do. Many times that notion is based on the last person they met with who called him- or herself a "financial advisor." Remember that? So you have to work, as quickly as you can, to dispel the perception that you are anything like their last (or current) advisor. The extent to which you can do that quickly is the extent to which you are likely going to win over that prospect. You've had a chance to see what we have used to quickly differentiate ourselves from our competitors. Just realize that it doesn't have to be complicated. Sometimes a simple story or way of explaining things can set you apart.

Leverage

I define this as having the right people on your team doing the right things. My guess is you probably already know your strengths. If you do not have much self-awareness, you had better find someone in your life who is not afraid to tell you the truth about your strengths and weaknesses. If you have the gift of self-awareness, you should also know what you are NOT good at. One key to success is surrounding yourself with the right people—people whose strengths complement yours. This way, as a group, you'll have all the bases covered.

Speaking of complementary associations, here are two extremes I have encountered: Once, my office was two-doors down from someone I would consider to be one of the most brilliant minds in the investment business. "Mike" had a keen sense of the market, knew everything there was to know about investing, and always seemed to make the correct market calls at precisely the right time. He was incredible; probably one of the brightest minds I have ever met. However, I remember being extremely confused as to why Mike was never in the top fifty percent of our office in production, even after more than twenty years in the business. In hindsight, I now know what he was missing was someone who was good at marketing and someone who could relate to people and understood the psychology of the sales process. Mike was a really smart guy, but he couldn't relate to people and couldn't communicate. I once heard Mike on a phone call explaining the current market conditions to a client in a manner that was appropriate for a group of students getting a PhD in economics, not for a recent retiree! He needed a translator—someone on his team who could take his brilliance and communicate his ideas on a fifth-grade level to his clients and prospective clients.

On the other end of the spectrum are advisors who have lots of personality, but little grasp of the industry. We all know someone in this business with whom we would love to go grab a drink after work. They are friendly and charismatic. Some even have personalities that are downright magnetic. But when you talk to them at length about anything business related, you question whether they could even spell standard deviation, let alone explain it to clients. Advisors with HUGE personalities but little technical depth need to surround themselves with the best technicians they can find. I have seen advisors try to keep clients happy solely based on their relationship, and it just doesn't work!

Leverage—in other words, using something to maximum advantage—can be accomplished in many ways. You might find leverage through your broker dealer in the form of money managers, investment products, training, and marketing materials. Your regional office may provide you with some support for compliance, marketing leads, office administration, licensed assistants, or a planning department. You may even have a para-planner of your own where you can literally groom someone to be your right-hand person. You may find leverage in a partner who complements the skills you bring to the table and with whom you can split business. You may outsource centers of influence like attorneys, CPAs, and money managers. Ultimately, leverage can help you reach more clients and make more money. You may just find yourself waking up more energized and excited than you ever thought you could be!

Systems and Processes

Do you like change? Do you really like change? Do you like it when the dentist office moves across the street and forgets to tell you? Do you like going to your favorite restaurant only to find they have changed their menu and your to-die-for dish is no longer being served? Studies have shown that most people prefer routines and thrive in environments where they know exactly what to expect next. As Erin explained, when your clients hire you, they are hoping for a certain experience. After they have been your clients for a while, they expect their experience with you or your firm to stay consistent. If they have been used to getting a call back within an hour and it takes three days to hear back from you, that is a problem. If your client is used to seeing that friendly receptionist who knows them by name each time they come in, yet finds a new person at your front desk who is less than friendly and seems inconvenienced by their arrival, that is an issue.

There are standards that you, as the leader of your business, must establish. Whatever standards you decide upon should be undergirded with systems and processes to make sure those standards are adhered to every single time. This applies to both what the client sees (the front stage) and what they don't see (the back stage). Consistency of experience is KEY. If the clients loved what they experienced on their first meeting with you, then they want to have that experience over and over and over again. The risk, when you add more people to your team, is that the client experience could drastically change based on how the people on your team treat them. If you make the commitment to expand your practice by adding staff, you must pair the people with solid systems and processes. By doing this, you can create a cohesive experience for the client that can be repeated over and over, no matter who is dealing with the client. Having your business run on predetermined systems and processes will result in happier clients and a happier team.

Not everything Erin and I have done in the Botsford Financial Group has worked. In fact, many things did not work. However, putting our heads together allowed us to quickly evaluate what was working and what was not. We were not afraid to be wrong, and when we failed, we did not wallow in our failure. Instead, we quickly got up and tried something different. To that end, there's no way we can outline in this book absolutely everything we have done that has contributed to our success. Instead, my hope is that the stories will inspire you to foster your own creativity. May you find your personal recipe for success! If we can do it, so can you!

Kay Lynn Mayhue
President, Botsford Financial Group